"In the daunting but essential struggle to transform the United Nations for its 21st century role as the core medium of multilateral discourse and governance, one could hardly wish for a more compelling team of reformers than the ones assembled in this volume. The analysis is incisive, the critiques constructive, and the proposals doable."

— *Ernie Regehr*
Director, Project Ploughshares

"Participants agreed that the adoption of the reforms suggested by Kofi Annan will not come easily and not all at once, but are nonetheless needed to restore the prestige and the credibility of the Organization."

— *Ambassador Adolfo Aguilar Zinser*
Former Permanent Representative of Mexico to the UN

"This volume brings together the views on UN reform of experienced senior diplomats and UN officials with outside observers, experts and academics. This yeasty brew not only reveals the intelligence and insights of these well-placed individuals but also the differing perspectives of insiders and outsiders, always with useful, and occasionally surprising, results. An extremely timely and important book, as the world focuses on how to recapacitate the UN for the global age."

— *Colin Bradford*
The Brookings Institution

IRRELEVANT OR INDISPENSABLE?
THE UNITED NATIONS IN THE
TWENTY-FIRST CENTURY

PAUL HEINBECKER AND PATRICIA GOFF, EDITORS

Wilfrid Laurier University Press

We acknowledge the support of the Canada Council for the Arts for our publishing program. We acknowledge the financial support of the Government of Canada through the Book Publishing Industry Development Program for our publishing activities. We acknowledge the financial support of the Centre for International Governance Innovation.

Library and Archives Canada Cataloguing in Publication Data

   Irrelevant or indispensable? : the United Nations in the
twenty-first century / Paul Heinbecker and Patricia Goff, editors.

Papers from a conference titled The UN: adapting to the 21st century,
   held April 4, 2005, in Waterloo, Ont.
Includes bibliographical references.
ISBN 978-0-88920-493-5 (paperback)

1. United Nations—Congresses.   2. Security, International—Congresses
3. Economic development—Congresses.   I. Heinbecker, Paul, 1941–
II. Goff, Patricia M.

JZ4984.I77 2005   341.23'01'3   C2005-903056-9

© 2005 Wilfrid Laurier University Press
Waterloo, Ontario, Canada
www.wlu.press.wlu.ca
This printing 2011

Cover design by P.J. Woodland, incorporating a graphic image by Alicia Rogers. Interior design by Catharine Bonas-Taylor.

Every reasonable effort has been made to acquire permission for copyright material used in this text, and to acknowledge all such indebtedness accurately. Any errors and omissions called to the publisher's attention will be corrected in future printings.

∞

Printed in Canada

MIX
Paper from
responsible sources
FSC
www.fsc.org   FSC® C021996

This book is dedicated to those whose security, prosperity, and dignity depend on a strong United Nations.

CONTENTS

Acknowledgments ix

List of Acronyms xi

1 Introduction 1
Paul Heinbecker and Patricia Goff

FROM IDEAS TO ACTION

2 The United Nations: Adapting to the Twenty-first Century 9
Louise Fréchette

3 The Millennium Project: From Words to Action 19
Jeffrey Sachs

4 UN Reform and the High-level Panel Report on Threats,
Challenges, and Change 25
Lord David Hannay

5 Implementing the Secretary General's Report,
"In Larger Freedom" 33
Bruce Jones

FREEDOM FROM WANT

6 The Monterrey Consensus: Developing the
Policy Innovations 43
Nitin Desai

7 Ensuring Adequate Resources to Meet the Millennium
Development Goals 63
John W. McArthur

FREEDOM FROM FEAR

8   **WMD and Terrorism: Can the UN Help to Keep the Genie in the Bottle? 79**
    Jayantha Dhanapala

9   **Legal and Legitimate Use of Force under the UN Charter: A Critical Analysis of the Report of the High-level Panel 89**
    Tom Farer

10 **Small Arms, Big Killers 105**
    Keith Krause

LIVING IN DIGNITY

11 **Freedom from Fear: Effective, Efficient, and Equitable Security 115**
    Ramesh Thakur

12 **The UN Reform Agenda and Human Rights 131**
    Kenneth Roth

INSTITUTIONAL INNOVATION

13 **The UN Security Council: Reform or Enlarge? 143**
    Edward C. Luck

14 **Working Better Together: Implementing the High-level Panel's Recommendations on Peacebuilding 153**
    Shepard Forman

MOBILIZING ACTION

15 **Making the Case for Change 169**
    Lloyd Axworthy

16 **Managing the Reform Agenda: A Call for Timely Action 177**
    Jean Ping

CONCLUSION

17 **The Way Forward 183**
    Paul Heinbecker

    Notes on Contributors 189

    Appendix: Conference Agenda 193

ACKNOWLEDGMENTS

In March of 2005, the Secretary General released his report on UN reform, *In Larger Freedom*. The leaders' summit, where he hopes member states will endorse his reform package, is scheduled to take place in September of 2005. For the proceedings of our April 2005 UN reform conference to have any impact on the debate in the ensuing months, we had to perform a feat of publishing magic that was only made possible by the very hard work of several people.

At the Centre for International Governance Innovation (CIGI), we would like to express our thanks to Jim Balsillie, Chairman of the Board. The Centre owes its existence to his vision and philanthropy. We would also like to recognize Michael Barnstijn and Louise MacCallum for their great generosity and their particular interest in UN governance work. John English, Executive Director of CIGI, was steadfast in his support. Sandy Rung and Caroline Khoubesserian were instrumental in the preparation of this manuscript.

At the Academic Council on the United Nations System (ACUNS), special thanks are owed to Alistair Edgar and John Allison. David Docherty at Wilfrid Laurier University (WLU) deserves special credit for encouraging the book very early on. Of course, there would be no book had there not been a conference, and we are very grateful to all the members of the CIGI, ACUNS, and WLU teams, too numerous to mention here, who worked so hard to make the conference a success. We are also indebted to all who attended the conference for their enthusiastic participation.

Wilfrid Laurier University Press registered their support for this project by the speed with which they brought it to press. We are especially grateful to Brian Henderson, Leslie Macredie, Carroll Klein,

Jacqueline Larson, and all the Press staff who worked so hard to get this manuscript out at a very busy time. Andrew Thompson did an excellent job on copy editing, showing great equanimity in the face of the timetable.

Finally, we thank the contributors to this volume, who agreed to revise their chapters in days, not weeks. We hope that their important and thought-provoking interventions will not fall on deaf ears.

LIST OF ACRONYMS

AU	African Union
BCPR	Bureau for Crisis Prevention and Recovery
BWC	Biological Weapons Convention
CAP	Compliance Assistance Program
CTBT	Comprehensive Test-Ban Treaty
CTC	Counter Terrorism Committee
CWC	Chemical Weapons Convention
DAC	Development Assistance Committee
DFID	United Kingdom's Department for International Development
DDR	Disarmament, Demobilization and Reintegration
DPKO	Department of Peacekeeping Operations
EAPC	Euro-Atlantic Partnership Council
ECOSOC	United Nations Economic and Social Council
EU	European Union
FAO	Food and Agricultural Organization
G-8	Group of 8 industrialized countries
G-20	Group of 20
G-77	Group of 77 developing countries
GATT	General Agreement on Trade and Tariffs
GNI	Gross National Income
HEU	Enriched Uranium
HIPC	Heavily Indebted Poor Countries
HLP	High-level Panel on Threats, Challenges and Change
HLPR	High Level Panel Report
IAEA	International Atomic Energy Agency
ICC	International Criminal Court

ICJ	International Court of Justice
IDA	International Development Association
IFIs	International Financial Institutions
IGOs	Inter-governmental Organizations
IMF	International Monetary Fund
INDs	Improvised Nuclear Devices
IPU	Inter-Parliamentary Union
LDCs	Least Developed Countries
MAP	Model Additional Protocol
MDGs	Millennium Development Goals
NAM	Non-Aligned Movement
NATO	North Atlantic Treaty Organization
NEPAD	New Partnership for Africa's Development
NGOs	Non-governmental organizations
NSG	Nuclear Suppliers Group
NPT	Nuclear Non-Proliferation Treaty
NTC	Nuclear Terrorism Convention
OAS	Organization of American States
ODA	Official Development Assistance
OPCW	Organization for the Prohibition of Chemical Weapons
P5	Existing five permanent members of the Security Council
PBSO	Peacebuilding Support Office
PRSPs	Poverty Reduction Strategy Papers
Prepcom	Preparatory Committee
PSI	Proliferation Security Initiative
R2P	*The Responsibility to Protect*
SC	United Nations Security Council; see also UNSC
SG	United Nations Secretary General
SRSG	Special Representative of the Secretary General
TRIPs	Trade-related Aspects of Intellectual Property Rights
UN	United Nations
UNDG	United Nations Development Group
UNDP	United Nations Development Programme
UNGA	United Nations General Assembly
UNICEF	United Nations International Children's Emergency Fund
USD	United States Dollars
WGTDF	Working Group on Trade, Debt and Finance
WHO	World Health Organization
WMDs	Weapons of Mass Destruction
WTO	World Trade Organization

PAUL HEINBECKER
PATRICIA GOFF

1 INTRODUCTION

International institutions are often forged in the fire of experience, responses to events that demonstrate what can happen when international cooperation breaks down. The United Nations (UN) is one of these organizations. In the wake of two catastrophic world wars within a thirty-year period, the victors of World War II convened fifty-one countries to fashion a collective security arrangement that would prevent in the second half of the twentieth century a repeat of the horrible events of the first half. Not surprisingly, the founders put into place an organization that reflected both the main political concerns and the distribution of power of the 1940s, as well as the lessons derived from the failure of the League of Nations.

Sixty years after the birth of the UN, the array of concerns has shifted and expanded. Collective security continues to be a central issue, but our answers to the question about the UN's collective security mandate, "security from what?" would differ substantially from the answers the founders might have offered in 1945. For example, civil wars and terrorism are much more likely to disrupt global security than great power war. Small arms or "dirty bombs" are of much greater concern for many than missiles and warheads. Furthermore, the major threat to the security of countless people is not violence or conflict. Indeed, for millions the major threat to well-being comes from poverty, disease, inequality, forced migration or environmental degradation. These latter threats ensure that the broad goal of development exists alongside security as central objectives for the United Nations today, objectives Secretary General Kofi Annan has conceptualized as "freedom from want" and "freedom from fear." Increasingly, it is becoming apparent that these goals will not be attained in isolation from each other. As the Secretary General has observed, "we will not enjoy development without security, we will not enjoy security without development, and we will not enjoy either without respect for human rights."[1]

The answer to the question "security for whom?" has also changed. Ethnic cleansing in the Balkans and genocide in Rwanda again demonstrate that states may be unwilling or unable to protect their citizens from security threats or might themselves be the threat. This sad realization has led to a broadening of the very notion of security, to include not only national security or the security of the state, but also human security, or the security of the individual. It has also led to the emerging norm that holds that, in the face of large-scale loss of life, the principle of non-intervention yields temporarily to the responsibility of the international community to protect the innocent. Sovereignty, after all, comprises both rights and responsibilities.

Just as the nature of our concerns has changed, so has the constellation of powerful actors on the global stage. In 1945, the United States and the Soviet Union were emergent powers, while Germany and Japan were defeated and devastated. In 2005, the United States is the sole superpower and the Soviet Union is no more. Japan is the second largest economic power in the world, Germany is at the centre of a new type of supranational organization; the European Union, and developing countries like China, Brazil, and India occupy positions of growing political and economic influence. These states operate alongside increasingly prominent private entities and civil society groups.

This shift in the distribution of power, accompanied by the emergence of new threats and concerns, means that the context within which the United Nations operates has changed dramatically since 1945. The need to adapt to twenty-first-century socio-political and economic realities is the strongest argument in favour of United Nations reform today. Current realities require the UN to be relevant to the security of the weak and the powerful; to be as effective at peace-building as it is at peacekeeping; to anticipate and respond to the transnational challenges of our time, while promoting and consolidating the rule of law. The United Nations remains indispensable to the preservation of peace and security, to the attainment of prosperity, and to the advancement of human rights, but its mandate, and the tools at its disposal to fulfill it, must be adapted to the changing times.

•   •   •

This volume assembles the papers and speeches that were delivered at a conference on United Nations reform, held in Waterloo, Ontario, Canada, in early April of 2005. The conference was the first to assemble practitioners, United Nations ambassadors, civil society representatives, and academics following the release of the Secretary General's report, *In Larger Freedom*, in March 2005. The Secretary General was, himself, responding to two reports that he had commissioned—one on security; the High-level Panel Report on Threats, Challenges, and Change, entitled *A More Secure World: Our Shared Responsibility*, delivered in December 2004; and one on development; the Report of the Millennium Project, entitled *Investing in Development: A Practical Plan to Achieve the Millennium Development Goals*, delivered in January 2005. The conference both responded to these reports and anticipated the summit due to take place in September 2005, uniting member states five years after the adoption of the Millennium Declaration. It is at that Summit that Secretary General Annan hopes that leaders will endorse the reform agenda outlined in *In Larger Freedom*.

The volume opens with an overview of the challenges of the reform process as articulated by the Deputy Secretary General of the United Nations, Madame Louise Fréchette. Madame Fréchette's perspective is followed by introductions to the three key reform reports by individuals who were instrumental in their preparation. Jeffrey Sachs presents the findings of the Millennium Project. He issues a call to action for developing countries to implement poverty eradication strategies and for developed countries to invest the requisite resources to help poor countries find their way out of the poverty trap they are in. Lord David Hannay outlines the key concerns of the High-level Panel on Threats, Challenges and Change and advocates a holistic and collective approach to reform. Bruce Jones clarifies many of the key components of the Secretary General's report, emphasizing the interconnections between security, development, and human rights, as well as institutional reform.

In his report, Secretary General Annan identifies four broad areas for reform and we adopt these four themes as an organizing framework for subsequent sections of this volume. Under the heading of "Freedom from Want," the Secretary General notes that great strides have been made in reducing poverty in the last twenty-five years, but much work is still to be done. He identifies a series of priorities for meeting the Millennium Development Goals (MDGs) by 2015, including MDG-based national development strategies in developing countries; donor country timetables for achieving the goal of allocating 0.7 percent of gross national income to official development assistance; the successful conclusion of the Doha development round of trade talks; debt relief for the poorest countries; new action on environmental sustainability; and reform of the international financial institutions.

In the chapters that follow, John McArthur reinforces the message that the Millennium Development Goals are achievable by 2015, but only if governments act now. He pays special attention to the promise of implementing the Millennium Project's "Quick Wins," as well as the need to "fast-track" developing countries that are ready to implement poverty eradication strategies in the near term. He further identifies specific roles that the United Nations can play to facilitate this process. Nitin Desai also takes up the theme of "Freedom from Want," but within the context of the agreement on development cooperation reached at the International Conference on Financing for Development, held in Monterrey, Mexico, in 2002. Desai emphasizes that a new consensus on development is emerging, but implementing it requires, among other things, resources and the reform of the international financial institutions—the International Monetary Fund, the World Bank, and the World Trade Organization—and their coordination with the United Nations to ensure a coherent and effective approach to international economic governance.

In *In Larger Freedom*, Secretary General Annan notes that we have not yet developed a security consensus akin to the development consensus, in large part because of the contradictions inherent in safeguarding sovereignty while also providing for the pre-emptive and preventive use of force in self-defence. He also urges member states to adopt a vision of security that seeks to assure everyone's security, acknowledging that infectious diseases, environmental disasters, and small arms can have consequences as catastrophic as more commonly recognized threats to security, such as war and terrorism.

In this vein, Jayantha Dhanapala's chapter addresses the role the United Nations can play in stemming the threat from weapons of mass destruction (WMDs) and terrorism. He argues in favour of a disaggregation of weapons of mass destruction to deal with nuclear, biological, and chemical weapons separately. Further, he notes there are steps to be taken, both in terms of pragmatic capacity-building, but also at the normative level, embracing the Secretary General's definition of terrorism. Tom Farer looks at the use of force with an eye to identifying what is legal and legitimate under the United Nations Charter. He argues that what is legitimate and what is legal may not always coincide and that a shift to human security may lead us to rethink the circumstances under which we resort to force. Keith Krause examines the complex question of how to stem the illegal use of small arms and light weapons. He argues that the UN has a crucial role to play in this, providing it starts from the recognition that any approach to the problem of small arms must confront a range of issues from organized crime to the destruction of surplus weapons stocks.

In Larger Freedom emphasizes the importance of recognizing that the freedom from fear and want is incomplete without the freedom to live in dignity. Essential to the security and development agendas is respect for the rule of law and human rights, as well as consolidation of democratic governance and the protection of the innocent. Secretary General Annan notes that there is an impressive framework of laws and norms in place that must be respected and implemented.

Ramesh Thakur explores the legitimacy and lawfulness of UN action within the context of *The Responsibility to Protect*, arguing that this emerging norm is the bridge that unites the "Freedom from Want" and "Freedom from Fear" agendas. Kenneth Roth discusses the Secretary General's proposals to reinvigorate the human rights mandate of the United Nations through the creation of a Human Rights Council. He advocates a Council of limited size, whose membership is prepared to promote human rights.

The UN reform agenda requires at least as much action on the part of member states as it requires of the institution itself. Nonetheless, the Secretary General places at the centre of his reform agenda efforts to strengthen existing organs, in particular, the Security Council. He also proposes innovative changes, such as a Peacebuilding Commission to fill a lacuna in the UN's instruments for preserving peace and preventing conflict.

Edward Luck takes up this issue in his chapter on Security Council reform. He counsels caution on this front, arguing that it may not be the time for such high-profile change, especially if doing so brings no guarantee that the UN will operate more efficiently or effectively as a result. Shepard Forman examines the Secretary General's proposal for a Peacebuilding Commission to address the needs of state failure and post-conflict reconstruction. He argues that the UN has a critical role to play and he lays out a series of recommendations to help it do so.

The final section of the volume includes chapters by Lloyd Axworthy and Jean Ping. Axworthy emphasizes the crucial need to engage member state publics in the reform process. Jean Ping, in his capacity as President of the General Assembly, outlines the timeline and major milestones on the road to the leaders' summit in September. Paul Heinbecker concludes the volume with a call to action.

Some of the chapters that follow were prepared in advance of the conference to be delivered as papers. Other chapters were delivered as keynote addresses or speeches. In the interest of preserving the thrust of the contributors' respective arguments, we kept them largely in their original form, rather than attempting to impose a uniform style on all of the chapters. Therefore, some chapters have scholarly references, while others do not. Some chapters have a more conversational tone, while others do not.

The United Nations is an extraordinarily broad organization, with a mandate that spans the entire gamut of human experience. The reform agenda is equally broad. Nevertheless, in a two-day conference, we found it necessary to focus our efforts on certain issues, regrettably de-emphasizing others. In this latter category, we find such significant topics as a sustainable environment, gender issues, natural disasters, and the role of regional organizations as UN partners. It is our fervent hope that this volume will not be read as suggesting that these topics are less important than the ones that get attention here. They are all central elements of the reform agenda, as the Secretary General makes clear in his report. This volume is one intervention in what we hope will be a constructive, frank, and ongoing conversation about UN reform and we look forward to other interventions that accentuate topics that we were unable to address.

NOTE

1   Kofi Annan, *In Larger Freedom: Towards development, security and human rights for all*. Report of the Secretary General (New York: United Nations, document A/59/2005, 21 March 2005), para. 17.

FROM IDEAS TO ACTION

2 THE UNITED NATIONS
ADAPTING TO THE TWENTY-FIRST CENTURY

I joined the United Nations on a wave of reform—indeed, the position that I occupy, that of Deputy Secretary General, was part of Kofi Annan's first reform package in 1997. The reforms put in place at that time did much to restore confidence in the organization—confidence that had been badly eroded, above all, by the UN's failures in Bosnia and Rwanda. Those reforms continued throughout the 1990s, and we introduced a second wave of reforms in 2002.

Thanks in part to these changes, the organization emerged from a prolonged funding crisis with the United States. I vividly remember the day when Senators Helms and Biden visited UN Headquarters with the Senate Foreign Relations Committee, and how that led to the implementation of the Helms-Biden Act, under which the US eventually paid off most of its arrears due to the UN in 2001.

I also recall the palpable optimism of the moment in September 2000 when member states adopted the Millennium Declaration—a remarkable document which showed widespread confidence that humanity could make measurable progress towards peace, security, disarmament, human rights, democracy, and good governance. And I think all of us who serve the United Nations were proud when, a year later, the Security Council responded swiftly and decisively to the terrorist attacks of 11 September 2001.

Today, however, it is difficult not to feel that we have, in some respects at least, slid back down the greasy pole to somewhere near the place where we started eight years ago. The organization has been deeply scarred by the divisions over the war in Iraq. Many who supported the war saw the Security Council's failure to authorize action as symptomatic of the UN's inability to provide a muscular response to today's threats. Many who opposed the war were disillusioned that the UN appeared helpless to prevent what they saw as a premature and dangerous war, fought on uncertain grounds. As a result—and notwithstanding the deployment by the Security Council of a host of new peacekeeping missions to stabilize other troublespots—at the very time where they were very divided over the Iraq issue, people on all sides experienced a crisis of confidence in the United Nations. The controversies surrounding the Oil-for-Food Program only added fuel to the fire, as did other failings in the conduct of staff and peacekeepers. Today the calls for reform are stronger than ever.

Once again, the Secretary General is leading the charge. In September 2003, he warned that the international community stood at a fork in the road, and then set up the High-level Panel (HLP) to put forward a new vision of collective security that could command the confidence of all states. It was also he who set up the Millennium Project, to give both rich and poor nations a plan of action to meet the Millennium Development Goals (MDGs).

Those two bodies produced their reports this winter, and two weeks ago, the Secretary General published his own report entitled, *In Larger Freedom*. That report offers member states a package of decisions which, taken together, could forge an effective multilateral response to the great challenges of our time, and make the United Nations itself an effective instrument of that response.

For some of our harshest critics, this is a futile exercise. They view the United Nations as a worn-out relic of a bygone era, inefficient and ineffective, corrupt and morally bankrupt—in short, next to useless. But if that is true, why do States entrust so many vitally important tasks to the United Nations? Why have they turned to it to spearhead an unprecedented global response to the Asian tsunami, and to the more recent earthquake in the region? Why did they call on the UN to help with the creation of an interim government in Iraq, and to provide technical assistance during the recent elections? Indeed, why do member states put more than 70,000 of their troops at the disposal of the United Nations to deploy in peacekeeping missions in four continents—which, I feel compelled to add, the UN does on the impressively small budget of around $4 billion a year.

I could, in fact, spend my entire speech listing all the things that the UN does, day in and day out, to save lives and help stabilize societies. But I won't. I could expound at length on how a UN framework brings legitimacy to international action and helps maximize global cooperation in pursuit of common goals. Again, I will spare you.

But I *will* take a minute to sing the praises of UN staff, because I cannot remain silent when I see their reputation being tarnished by the misbehaviour of a few of their colleagues, or by the shortcomings, real or imagined, of their leaders, mine included. The vast majority of UN staff are very talented, highly skilled, and deeply devoted to the organization, and many pursue that devotion at great personal cost. Some have even paid with their lives. Many more pay every day by accepting the disruption of their family life, and constant shuttling from war zone to war zone. I am proud to work with them, and I do not for one minute accept the caricature of the Secretariat which nowadays masquerades as fact.

But I fully agree that reforms—bold and far-reaching policy reform and institutional reforms—are both urgent and necessary. The Secretary General's report contains recommendations on the changes that he believes must be made if the organization is to provide an effective collective response to all the threats we face—from deadly weapons and catastrophic terrorism to killer diseases and life-threatening poverty—if we are to advance development, security and human rights with equal determination. Reform is necessary on four sets of issues—in basic policy, in the instruments at our disposal, in intergovernmental institutions, and in the management of the Secretariat.

Let me take policy first. There, reform is urgent and necessary because our member states remain deeply divided on key issues—divisions which paralyze collective action and cripple multilateral institutions. They have been divided on what the most important threats are to international peace and security; on how to fight terrorism effectively; on the need to save civilians from massive atrocities inside sovereign states; whether or when it is right to use force in the face of non-imminent threats.

If we are to overcome these divisions, the starting point must be a broad vision of collective security—one which accepts that all threats that cause death on a large scale or undermine states as the basic unit of the international system are common threats, requiring a collective response from humanity as a whole. The Report of the Secretary General offers important policy recommendations for consideration by member states to give effect to that vision, including:

- A strategy for fighting terrorism that includes a place for coercive measures, of course, but goes far beyond them. At its centre would be a comprehensive anti-terrorism convention based on an agreed definition. Last week's agreement on a convention against nuclear terrorism is an important step in this direction.

- The report also recommends adoption and application by the Security Council of principles which would guide decisions on the use of force.
- And endorsement of the norm of the "responsibility to protect," which Canada, of course, has done so much to promote, as a basis for collective action against genocide, ethnic cleansing, or crimes against humanity, when governments themselves are either unwilling or unable to protect their citizens.

I must stress that mere agreement on these basic policy changes is no panacea. There would still be plenty of hard-fought negotiations, and plenty of issues on which member states would find it difficult to agree. But agreement on the Secretary General's proposals would give us vital tools to promote consensus, and a much better chance of reaching decisions that command wide respect.

Second, let me turn to the instruments at our disposal. Reform is urgent and necessary because some of them have not kept pace with changing times.

The dangers of nuclear proliferation are a clear example. While the Nuclear Non-Proliferation Treaty (NPT) has prevented far more states from acquiring nuclear weapons than was ever expected, the spread of nuclear technology has exacerbated a long-standing tension arising from the fact that the technology required for civilian nuclear fuel can also be used to develop nuclear weapons. To address this tension, the Secretary General's report recommends strengthening the verification authority of the International Atomic Energy Agency (IAEA) through universal adoption of the Model Additional Protocol (MAP).

Tougher inspections, however, are not enough. Unless we want to live in a far more dangerous world, we must also create viable incentives for states to voluntarily forego the development of sensitive aspects of the fuel cycle. All of this should occur in the context of a revitalized regime in which our commitments to both non-proliferation and disarmament transcend old fault lines, and are expressed not just in word but in deed. Swift negotiation of a fissile material cut-off treaty should be a top priority. So too should be a sustained commitment to the moratorium on nuclear testing and the entry into force of the Comprehensive Test-Ban Treaty (CTBT).

Another example of an instrument that needs updating is UN peacekeeping. The reforms undertaken following the Brahimi report have given us clearer doctrine and better peacekeeping capability. But we still lack adequate standby arrangements to enable quick deployment, with the necessary strategic reserve. And we must develop an interlocking system of peacekeeping capacities that will enable the United Nations to work with relevant regional organizations in predictable and reliable partnerships.

The third set of issues relates to our intergovernmental institutions. There, reform is urgent and necessary because a number of our decision-making bodies are insufficiently representative, or unfocussed, or ill-suited to dealing with new challenges.

Let me start with the Security Council. A more broadly representative Security Council, one that better reflects the geopolitical realities of today, would be more authoritative, and therefore more effective. This view is widely shared among the membership. But as is well known, disagreement on the details of enlargement of the Council has stymied progress towards a resolution. The Secretary General believes that member states should, for the sake of the institution, take a decision on this issue before September. Of course, consensus on such a vital matter would be much preferable. But the best must not become the enemy of the good.

In the last decade and a half, the role of the United Nations in peacebuilding has become one of its most important contributions to collective security. Peacebuilding draws in many actors, both within the UN system and outside it, and needs to work to strengthen security, rule of law, human rights and development. But there is a gaping hole in the United Nations institutional machinery—no part of the intergovernmental system draws these strands together to effectively address the challenges of helping countries with the transition from war to lasting peace.

That is why the Secretary General has embraced the High-level Panel's recommendation to create a Peacebuilding Commission, which he believes would improve planning and coordination, and help sustain political will and financial support for long-term peacebuilding efforts. The Commission's membership should include a sub-set of member states of both the Security Council and the Economic and Social Council, and draw in troop contributors, major donors, relevant regional actors, international financial institutions, as well as countries concerned.

Equally far-reaching is the Secretary General's proposal to create a Human Rights Council to sit alongside the Security Council and the Economic and Social Council. While the Commission on Human Rights does important work, states have too often sought membership not to strengthen human rights but to protect themselves against criticism or to criticize others. The Commission meets for six weeks a year, pursuing an agenda that is extremely selective and politicized, using methods that are extremely adversarial. A Human Rights Council would consecrate human rights as a central pillar of the UN, on a par with security and development. The Council could sit throughout the year, and periodically review and promote, in a more systematic and objective way, respect for *all* human rights in *all* countries. Its ultimate form and function is, of course, a matter for discussion and decision among member states—but I believe they must tackle this important institutional reform without delay.

Finally, let me turn to management of the Secretariat. Reform is urgent and necessary because the UN's internal management clearly lacks sufficient transparency, accountability and integrity, despite major reforms since 1997—including the overhaul of a number of departments, better budget and management systems, and, more recently, a complete transformation of our staff security system.

The challenges of managing a large and complex international organization are manifold. The UN system is hybrid in nature—part foreign service, part conference-servicer, part operational agency, part research institute. It has fragmented administrative oversight, and member states exert heavy political pressure, often seeking to co-manage the organization alongside the Secretary General as Chief Administrative Officer. And the organization is probably the most multicultural employer in the world—which makes it an exciting place to work, but also brings with it its own set of management challenges.

Some of our problems stem from these unique challenges—but none of them can excuse systemic poor management or ethical lapses among staff. We are gravely concerned at the failures brought to light in the Oil-for-Food Program, and appalled at the allegations of sexual abuse by UN staff and peacekeepers in the Democratic Republic of the Congo and elsewhere.

When problems come to light, you must act aggressively to fix them—and that's what we're doing. The Secretary General is moving swiftly on issues within his own purview—for instance, new protections for whistleblowers, wider access to information, higher standards to avoid conflicts of interest or corruption by senior officials, and action to hold managers to account.

In his report, the Secretary General asks the member states to do their part to help reform the Secretariat, including by reviewing all mandates more than five years old and all the rules governing the deployment of both budgetary and human resources, and by authorizing a one-time staff buy-out. Without this kind of rationalization and reorientation, the Secretariat will not be able to meet the range of demands placed on it by member states.

Of course, agreement on reforms of any kind is useless if they simply amount to promises that are not put into practice. There is no clearer or more urgent example of this than the development agenda, where we have plenty of consensus but too little implementation.

Three years ago, at Monterrey, developed and developing countries struck a bargain. If we are to meet the Millennium Development Goals (MDGs) by 2015, we must make sure that this bargain is kept. From developing countries, we need real commitments to good governance, and comprehensive national strategies to meet the MDGs by 2015. From developed countries, we need the leadership to achieve a breakthrough in the Doha round of trade negotiations, and an immediate beefing up of resources for development, coupled with the establishment of timetables to meet the target of providing 0.7 percent of gross national income in development assistance by 2015.

With this kind of action, the MDGs *are* achievable—indeed, many countries are on track to achieve some of these goals. But many others, particularly in Africa, are falling behind, and need a combination of domestic reform and international assistance. Five years after the MDGs were propounded, and ten years away from the target date, 2005 is the year when all States must begin to meet their commitments to save people from destitution, starvation, and killer diseases.

As you know, the Secretary General has asked member states to view these proposals as a package—not a take-it-or-leave-it package, but a package which has some basic planks which need to be preserved. The challenges our world faces cannot neatly be separated into little boxes, one reading "threats to the rich world," and another reading "dangers for the poor." When threats are inter-linked, responses must be too. We will not enjoy development without security, we will not enjoy security without development, and we will not enjoy either without respect for human rights. All must be the subject of far-reaching decisions in September.

I have no illusions that achieving reforms on this scale is a simple proposition. Some big issues are on the table—some have been around for many years, others are before member states for the first time. A lot of political will is required if the September summit is to bear fruit.

But I firmly believe that success is possible, for two reasons. First, because the United Nations has, in fact, been able to change enormously over its sixty-year history. The founders of the organization could hardly have imagined that there would be a High Commissioner for Human Rights, for instance, that we would be fully engaged with a broad cross-section of civil society, that we would have troops keeping the peace in over a dozen sovereign States, or, indeed, that the UN would have obliged one of its members to accept weapons inspectors on its territory. All of these developments point to the organization's ability to adapt itself, and to look beneath the surface of states and nations to the peoples in whose name the Charter was adopted. The UN may be a leopard that doesn't easily change its spots. But even though it looks the same, it has, in fact, become a very different animal.

Second, I believe that there is, at this time, widespread understanding of the implications of not acting—coupled with a welcome effort, on the part of key member states, to rebuild bridges of understanding that were pretty badly damaged in recent years. There is a real sense that faith and confidence in the multilateral route will only endure if people see that the system can actually deliver. Member states are, I believe, seized of the necessity for reform, as are we in the Secretariat. The reform agenda has now gone beyond diplomatic cocktail party chatter in New York, and has begun to register in world capitals and among the general public. The Secretary General intends, among other things, to dispatch high-level envoys to capitals in the coming period to build on that momentum.

All this is well and good—but let me conclude with the most important point of all. The success or failure of this effort will not depend on the Secretary General alone, and this reform is not about him. Its fate will depend, ultimately, on the decisions of member states, and its purpose is to set the organization on a more effective and hopeful course. September's summit is the chance for world leaders to take decisions that can help halve global poverty in the next ten years, reduce the threat of war, terrorism and deadly weapons of mass destruction, advance human dignity in every land, and reform the United Nations with a speed and boldness not seen in its sixty-year history. They must use it, or lose it.

I am confident that leaders will use this opportunity, and that people everywhere will reap the benefits. Member states now have before them a set of practical proposals for pragmatic decisions. From such beginnings could emerge a visionary change of direction for our world.

3 THE MILLENNIUM PROJECT
FROM WORDS TO ACTION

The Millennium Development Goals (MDGs) were adopted following the Millennium Assembly in September 2000. In 2002, Secretary General Kofi Annan asked me to direct the UN Millennium Project, which has identified practical ways to achieve the MDGs by 2015 in all countries affected by extreme poverty.

The UN Millennium Project, organized around ten task forces, brought together more than 250 development leaders from around the world, including scientists, academics, practitioners, and business and NGO leaders. Additionally, we had tremendous support from all the relevant UN agencies and special programs and funds by means of a UN expert group that engaged the International Monetary Fund (IMF), the World Bank, the Food and Agricultural Organization (FAO), UN Development Programme (UNDP), the United Nations Children's Fund (UNICEF), World Health Organization (WHO), and all the other agencies with tremendous expertise and a crucial role to play in poverty reduction. The project worked for nearly three years to complete its diagnosis and analysis, and it launched its reports on 17 January. Those reports address the many aspects of the MDGs: fighting hunger; fighting child and maternal mortality; fighting AIDS, tuberculosis, and malaria; guaranteeing access to essential medicines; water and sanitation; the role of science and technology; and the challenges of slum dwellers.

The main report is titled *Investing in Development: A Practical Plan to Achieve the Millennium Development Goals*. The two operative words are "investing" and "practical," because they emphasize that the MDGs can still be achieved in any country in the world with extreme poverty. For the dozens of countries that are not on course to achieve the MDGs, the difference comes down to investments in proven technologies and systems to address the challenges of extreme poverty. For example, to control child mortality, one needs clinics that can provide essential health services, safe drinking water and so forth. The UN Millennium Project has identified hundreds of specific investments in many categories. Unfortunately, these investments are simply are not being made at scale right now in the poorest countries in the world.

We have made a diagnosis that illustrates several reasons for the lack of these investments. Many people think that corruption is the primary cause. Corruption plays a role in many countries, and in some it plays an egregious role. While it is clear that corruption interferes with development, claiming that corruption is the obstacle to development radically over-simplifies the situation in dozens of impoverished countries around the world. In many countries, the most important obstacle is extreme poverty itself. Even relatively well-governed, extremely poor countries cannot mobilize the resources needed to undertake the core investments necessary to escape from the poverty trap. Without breaking the poverty trap, good governance alone is insufficient. This is where the help of the rich world, long promised and chronically under-delivered, becomes so vital. To the extent that countries are trapped in poverty, meaning that they lack the domestic resources needed to make the investments to address the challenges of the MDGs, the rich world must honour its commitments and obligations to help provide the financing necessary to make those investments possible. These promises were first made over four decades ago.

In addition to poor governance and the poverty trap, there are two other categories that I think require attention. One concerns the pockets of poverty that exist in remote areas of otherwise reasonably well-functioning economies. This stems from the geographical isolation of far-removed areas that need regional development strategies to rise out of extreme poverty. Finally, there are policy issues that even relatively well-governed countries are neglecting to address. Specifically, these include issues such as safe childbirth. Hundreds of thousands of women die each year while in labour or from resulting complications. We found a pervasive neglect of this issue by governments around the world, even in middle-income countries, with dangerous shortfalls in emergency obstetrical care. This is not the product of bad governance, but rather of a lack of knowledge of specific steps that can be taken.

One core recommendation is that countries should prepare poverty reduction strategies—including Poverty Reduction Strategy Papers

(PRSPs) where appropriate—that are based on the MDGs. Instead of simply evoking the MDGs as general goals, the MDGs ought to be linked to actual investment programming and the medium-term expenditure framework. In turn, official development assistance must be linked to the medium-term expenditure framework to ensure that countries do not fail to achieve the MDGs simply because they lack financing. Another core recommendation is that rich countries follow through on their commitments made in Monterrey in 2002 and repeatedly in previous decades. Only much larger levels of official development assistance can let countries realize the MDGs. This also calls for a very different role of the IMF. Rather than advising cash-strapped countries not to invest in healthcare and clinics, roads, power, ports, and other forms of infrastructure, the IMF ought to help countries achieve a macroeconomic framework based on the MDGs. That requires a reversal of business-as-usual; instead of telling developing countries to do less, the IMF will need to tell donors to do more. A truly goal-based system would have the IMF championing the cause of each developing country as it seeks the promised official development assistance. In many cases, the IMF already calls for more aid, but it needs to be more forceful, more visible, and more upfront about the link between official development assistance and achieving the MDGs.

National launches of the UN Millennium Project report have now taken place in around eighty countries. It was warmly received by international leaders, the African Union (AU) countries, the Group of 77 (G-77) and the vast majority of the high-income countries as well. It received similar strong endorsements from UN agencies, the Bretton Woods institutions, and others. What has won broad support is the concept of targeted, quantifiable diagnostics and investment programs linked to fiscal policies and development assistance. The Secretary General has clearly stated that the UN Millennium Project has provided a clear plan of action to achieve the MDGs.

So where are we now? We are looking for implementation and to move beyond words. That is the hardest part of the international system. We need all rich countries to commit to 0.7 percent of GNP in official development assistance on a timetable. While every country has already committed to the target, many countries, including Canada, Japan, and the United States, are not on a specific timetable to achieve it. Canada needs a timetable to reach 0.7 percent no later than 2015. It was a Canadian, Lester Pearson, whose "Partners in Development" report in 1969 put the 0.7 percent target before the General Assembly.

The United States gave the least official development assistance as a share of wealth of any rich country in 2003. If it continues on its current course, spending roughly half a trillion dollars on the military, and only sixteen billion dollars on development assistance, of which only a fraction goes to Africa, the MDGs will not be achieved, and the world will be rendered less secure.

The Secretary General was very clear in his call to action, and I think we need to get real results. Just recently, the Blair Commission for Africa found an absorptive capacity in Africa of tens of billions of dollars, and this mirrored the findings of the UN Millennium Project. The consensus of the world has grown clear: the time to act is now. Countries must be assured that their MDG-based strategies will be supported. A lack of donor financing must not be the barrier to development. Too frequently, countries put forward plans that are not financed. The donors can continue to short-change their partners in development, or they can follow through on their commitments.

The UN Millennium Project also called for a number of "Quick Wins," as did the Secretary General. The Quick Wins are actions that can have an extremely beneficial effect on human well-being immediately. One of the most dramatic would be to get malaria under control in the next three years through the mass distribution of insecticide-treated bed nets and the mass distribution of effective combination therapies, the new medicines of choice for fighting malaria. We must combine the bed nets with the combination drugs and indoor residual spraying, as well as with community-based training of community health workers and proper diagnostics. This can be done quickly, and we could save more than one million children a year who die of malaria.

Another Quick Win will spur local food productivity and apply it towards school meals programs on a massive scale, using locally produced food rather than food aid coming from abroad. We believe the combination of higher inputs of water, fertilizer, and seed at the local level in Africa, combined with universal school meals in hunger hotspots, could change the face of rural farming and dramatically enable and encourage children to attend school. Adequate nutrition will improve performance at school, and increased food productivity will reduce the necessity of their staying at home to assist with farming. This is a Quick Win that ought to occur within three years.

We also called for the elimination of user fees for health and education, because we know the user fees are rationing services to the poorest of the poor, keeping children out of schools, and families out of clinics. If donors made up the financing gap, this situation could be corrected quickly.

Donor countries have promised debt cancellation but failed to deliver it. One hundred percent debt cancellation for countries that require increased aid to meet the MDGs is vital.

The year 2005 is critical. We are approaching the Group of 8 (G-8) Summit in July and the important high-level summit at the UN in September. We desperately need action this year, and the United Nations must show that we can move from words to actions. There is no more opportune and urgent need to do that than in the area of fighting poverty, disease, and hunger. We have crafted a practical plan of action. I think it is clear what needs to be done. The role of Canada in this is clear—Canada must set a timetable to reach 0.7 percent and work with other countries to ensure that the MDGs are achieved on a global scale. I believe that the stakes are so high that this will be done, and that the people gathered today are committed to that effort. I look forward to Canada's great leadership in this endeavour.

4 UN REFORM AND THE HIGH-LEVEL PANEL REPORT ON THREATS, CHALLENGES, AND CHANGE

This conference is taking place at a very good moment and it's just when we should be taking stock of the UN Reform agenda. The cards are already all on the table, some might argue, rather too many cards, but I don't believe so myself because we are dealing with extremely complex matters and it doesn't help to simplify them excessively.

You've got the Report of the High-level Panel (HLP), the joint views from fifteen other colleagues from all around the world. You have Jeffrey Sachs's report which he has introduced with great eloquence and you have the Secretary General's (SG) own contribution which drew the threads of these reports together and identified the agenda that needed to be addressed by heads of government in September. I underline that because I think that it was absolutely essential the SG indicated the areas that needed to be addressed in September and I think we shouldn't spend too much time on his rather vexed reference to packages.

It's also a watershed, this meeting, between what has been happening the last four months, a very lively debate, livelier and wider in world terms I think than what has taken place in most people's living memories about the UN's system and how it works and how it ought to work in the future, and the move into a period of negotiation which now needs to get under way if there is to be a reasonable harvest in September. Now, I have been around a lot, and I do apologize for the fact that my travels since the High-level Panel Report have mainly been devoted to what I would call my parish, which is Western Europe and North America. I therefore do not, for one minute, wish to suggest that what I say reflects the reactions there have been, more widely; many of the meetings I have gone to have had representatives from Africa, Asia, and Latin America.

One thing that has struck me during these thousands of miles I have been traveling and advocating the High-level Panel's report has been a contrast between the reactions to it in Europe and Canada and those in the United States. There has been a marked discrepancy in the reactions. In Europe and Canada, on the whole, people seem, governments seem, to be anxious to get on with the reform agenda as it has been identified and as it has been prescribed in the HLP Report and the SG's report. In the US, there is a lot more existential questioning of the UN and there is of course a forcefully promoted, anti-UN agenda. Let's face it, there are two quite different opinions and it is important to keep them apart and not to get into a situation where you think that every criticism made by every American is designed to do down the United Nations. It isn't: it is designed to make the UN a better place too, but they come at it from a bit of a different angle, which is not surprising given the nature of the world power balance as it is now.

Second, I have come across a great deal of what I call loose talk of grand bargains. Now let me be very clear on this; I and the panel on which I served are quite clear. You have to have a broad security agenda that encompasses poverty, organized crime, environment, disease, and so on, as well as the more obvious issues of weapons of mass destruction, terrorism, and state failure. You have to have this broad agenda and proceed across the whole of that agenda if you are going to have any chance of producing a more secure and more equitable world. But that is a bit different from saying that one part of the agenda belongs as it were to the developing countries and if the developed countries put enough in the kitty, then they will graciously (the developing countries), agree to do something on security. Nor do I think that the developed countries should be saying that what they do on development depends on what developing countries agree to on security. I believe that to be conceptually—and in every other way— a flawed concept, and I would argue very, very strongly that we should not get into it. You will understand from what I say that I do not disagree with the view that there has to be a major advance on both sides of this equation if we are to make progress, but not because one part of the world does it for the other part of the world and vice versa. And I think it will be much better if, in the run-up to the September summit, there wasn't too much talk about this grand bargain but a lot more talk about how to move the whole agenda forward in a substantive way.

Third, we do have a problem, identified straightaway by the High-level Panel: a risk that the extremely important issue of Security Council enlargement becomes a cuckoo in the nest which expels all the other proposals and which in the cacophony of contrary views on this subject marginalizes the other issues. That would be very damaging for the UN if it were to happen.

I do not underestimate the importance of Security Council enlargement. I am strongly, as the other members of the panel were, in favour of it, and I am glad that the SG has proposed that an attempt should be made to settle that matter in advance of September in the General Assembly by means of a vote. I support both of those propositions, but I do think we need to be on our guard against it displacing the discussion of the policies the UN needs to have in the future as well as the sort of institutions it needs to have to implement those policies.

Fourth, one of the elements I picked up in my traveling, and that is not something you need to travel very far to find, you can find it just by walking out on First Avenue in New York, is the kind of insidious reductive process that all UN reform proposals go through by which everyone starts on day one and says these are wonderful proposals and then on day two and three they start clearing their throat and saying but, and then start pulling bits away here and pulling bits away there, and before you know where you are you end up in September with a wonderful communiqué full of warm words and no effective decisions.

So these are the four risks and tensions that I have identified out there. I believe they are all surmountable and manageable but you do need to be on your guard against them if you are genuinely trying to move forward this agenda.

How should we respond to these risks of diversion and reduction? Well, I was interested to see that when the United States, the President of the United States, put forward his proposal for a new Ambassador at the UN, the Secretary of State used a phrase which she seemed to have purloined from the European Union when she said that she favoured effective multilateralism. I think the key to narrowing this gap between the United States on the one hand and European countries and Canada on the other is to focus on this phrase and to put flesh on those bones.

What do we mean by effective multilateralism? How do we set about achieving it? Will we get all the way? Probably not. Will we get some of the way and build a consensus? Yes, I believe it can be done.

Then, as I say, I think we should forget about grand bargains. We have got to get stuck in and address the whole agenda of the High-level Panel and the Sachs agenda and we've got to come up with results; but don't let's have a pair of scales in which we put so much for the one side and that gets you so much for the other side. That will be, I think, very self-destructive

On the enlargement of the Security Council, as I say, I support the SG's proposal. I think it really is important to not set up a lot of cross-linkages and not to indulge in excessive hype. I think we all need to understand this is a very important issue for all the membership and it's a particularly important issue for a number of substantial countries who believe it is time they became permanent members of the Security Council, a view which I happen to share. But I do think it is important that that is not overdone, and that it is understood that those countries as well as other countries have the same stake in the well-being of the organization as a whole, whether or not the Security Council is enlarged.

And then, I think we do need from now onwards—and here, Mr. President, it's very much in your hands—to push forward the preparations and to build up the political support for decisions in September. The SG's idea, which I believe he is going to effect early this week by appointing some distinguished political figures from the different regions in the world to help him in the process of shaping up the September decisions, is a good one. I hope the various regional meetings that will take place, the European Union, the G-8, African Union, and many others all around the world will in the next two or three months really address this agenda seriously and make an impact because that is important.

Taking stock of the main items in this reform agenda as it looks now, I won't say anything more about the MDGs because Jeffrey Sachs has spoken eloquently about them. He did not speak about some other items that are on what I would call the economic and social side of the reform agenda but which are extremely important. Trade is one of them, of course, with the Doha Round having been pulled back from the brink of failure after Cancun, now on the rails again heading for a ministerial meeting in Hong Kong in December. We all know that it cannot be brought yet to a final conclusion but it needs to take another substantial step towards a conclusion which the SG believes and the panel believes ought to be in 2006. That may be optimistic but I don't think a set timetable is an unreasonable idea for trade negotiations as they have a tendency otherwise to go on forever.

On the environment, I do actually think that we are at a point where the dialogue of the deaf, which has been going on since the Kyoto Protocol was signed (and now of course has entered into force), may be becoming a little bit less deaf than it was. It's absolutely crucial that this year is the start of a new dialogue. We are not going to get new decisions this year, let's not kid ourselves, but we could get off onto a new footing. The G-8 meeting in Gleneagles, together with the meetings with a wide range of countries which will take place at the same time, could be a first step down the road towards a new effort in the environmental field that is desperately needed, for which we have a little bit of time since the Kyoto Timetable runs out in 2012; but it mustn't be rushed. We must not fall back into a dialogue of the deaf.

Then looking more directly at the High-level Panel proposals, on the issue of terrorism, I really believe the agenda is pretty clear now. The SG made, in my view, an absolutely first-class speech in Madrid three weeks ago, in which he set out the comprehensive strategy which the High-level Panel had called for. I have not heard any voices raised against his definition of that strategy, which is a very cogent one, and which addresses not only the symptoms of terrorism but the causes as well. The sooner we get on and back his strategy, the better. On specifics, I think that an unfilled need is to come to a common definition of terrorism against innocent civilians, a definition which we have searched for and so far failed to find. The world needs that, not principally for legal reasons but for political reasons. So we make it clear that as in the nineteenth century, when we finally, belatedly, outlawed piracy and slavery, so we are now going to outlaw terrorism in the form of targeting innocent non-combatants. That will have an enormously positive effect on a whole range of issues, including, I would say, the Middle East peace process, which is gradually beginning to show signs of revival.

Then on proliferation: there is a huge agenda there. We are about to go into a difficult non-proliferation review conference. It's going to be a struggle to avoid having that show as much discord as it does agreement. But it's important that it does move forward and that the United Nations system moves forward in this area, because the non-proliferation regimes, elaborate as they are, are in a state of some fragility at the moment and there is a real risk in the next few years of breakouts both in the nuclear and in the biological field, chemical less likely. If we don't make that effort now, it may be a great deal more difficult to handle these issues further down the road.

So the proposals put forward by the panel and put forward by the SG, making the Additional Protocol of the International Atomic Energy Agency (IAEA) a kind of gold standard which every country is held to, strengthening the Proliferation Security Initiative (PSI), trying to introduce a system that guarantees countries with bona fide civil nuclear programs access to enrichment and reprocessing facilities without the need to construct them themselves and thus become possessed of what everyone now knows is the shortcut to fissile material for weapons uses. These are really important proposals which need to be proceeded with. And it is absolutely essential that at the biological weapons meeting next year, we turn away from the deadlock and do-nothing situation that has prevailed for the last two or three years and get particularly involved in the question of inspection and the question of protection—protection, of course, raising the usual problem that the richer countries of the world are a great deal more likely to be able to protect themselves against biological weapons than the poorer and that is not an acceptable situation.

Then there is the issue of regional organizations. The High-level Panel and SG have taken a major step forward to make use of a section of the UN Charter which has been there for sixty years but which has never been properly used. I am delighted that the SG has now stated that he will accept the recommendation and will start to work up memoranda of understanding with any regional organization that has the capability to get involved in conflict prevention and peace operations so as to discuss and to channel exchanges of information, logistical support, training, and so on. I think it's also very good that he has endorsed our proposal that there needs to be a ten-year program of capacity building for the African Union, because the African Union has shown great willingness to move forward in this area but it does have severe limitations and constraints on resources. It is essential that the member states should be prepared on a case-by-case basis to back a regional peace operation with assessed contributions on the whole membership. If we want regions to do more, it is no good expecting regions like Africa, which are short of resources, to do that unless we are prepared to back them with our resources, not just encouraging words.

On the use of force we have put forward some guidelines. I insist on guidelines, as we are not trying to rewrite international law. We are not trying to lay down a push-button certainty of how to deal with a situation on the use of force. The panel recognizes, and the SG recognizes, that that will remain a case-by-case decision for the SC except where the unchanged provisions of Article 51 legitimize a forceful reaction in the event of an attack or threat of an imminent attack as defined by international law. The guidelines we put forward, as I say, are not designed to be international law; they are designed to increase the clarity and transparency with which the SC moves to decisions. They are designed to achieve a greater predictability and some degree of deterrence because if you know what is likely to happen then it is less likely, though not impossible, that the situation will move to one where force has to be used. And they should include the "responsibility to protect" in the international community, where a state is unwilling or unable to protect its own citizens from abuses of international humanitarian law. So I hope those principles and guidelines will be endorsed but not, as I say, in terms of new international law, properly speaking.

Then lastly, I mention the issue of Secretariat reform, where the SG has put forward some important proposals. Secretariat reform is not only important in functional terms; in the circumstances we live in now, it is absolutely vital in political terms.

There is one other thing I meant to refer to, which was the Peacebuilding Commission, the proposal to try and deal with state failure by having a much more structured approach to post-conflict peacebuilding. We will be waiting now for the SG to propose the precise details for that, which would enable it to be decided in September. I think this has been a huge gap in the UN's armory and I was pleased with how positive a response the proposal has received. The only thing I would say in mild complaint is that I do think that the pressure brought to bear on the SG and which led him to drop from the Peacebuilding Commission any concern with early warning and the first signs of state failure, was misguided. I think it was a pity, and I think the people who pressed him to remove early warning from the proposal were acting against their own interests.

I will give a bottle of champagne to anyone who can give me the name of a country that appeared on the agenda of the SC which would not have been better handled if it had appeared on that agenda earlier than it actually did. The reality is that governments are intensely anxious not to be brought into an international discussion of their problems, even when it may very well be that it is only through an international discussion and international support from the financial institutions and so on that they are going to be able to check the slide towards state failure. I accept what the SG has done. I just think that somewhere along the line, some people might find what I am saying is not entirely wide of the mark and perhaps then some adjustments will be made.

Now that is enough from me. I would just say this: there are a lot of the High-level Panel proposals and the proposals in Jeffrey Sachs's report which have not found their way into the September agenda, because the SG has rightly put forward an agenda which is doable and which is manageable and is not overburdened with detail. But a lot of those proposals are really important ones, and I hope that they will not be forgotten. I think it's in the interest of all those people around this room, whether they be non-governmental organizations (NGOs) or representatives of governments, to see that they are followed up. Proposals like the financing on assessed contributions of demobilization and disarmament in peace operations, proposals like the formalization of all the rules and procedures and changes that were made at the SC in the last fifteen years to make it more transparent, more responsive to the wider membership and which the panel proposed, should now be turned into formal rules of procedure. I could go on with a whole lot more. But what I am saying is that it is important not to forget about those areas which are below what you might call the horizon of visibility for heads of state and government in September. Well, there is plenty here to talk about in the next two days, and there is plenty to negotiate in the next four months. I hope that's the sort of basis on which we will move ahead.

5 IMPLEMENTING THE SECRETARY GENERAL'S REPORT, "IN LARGER FREEDOM"

Thank you very much, and thank you to Paul in particular for the invitation to be here today for this meeting. I have a fairly easy job because I get to rest on Jeff Sachs's and David Hannay's work in introducing the security and development aspects of the report before us. I'll try to be fairly brief because much of what I had intended to say was already covered to some extent by the Deputy Secretary General last night or by David just now in talking about some of the broader issues. But I will try to suggest what it is that the SG's report does in building on those previous reports and in adding a couple of dimensions. So I will make four broad points, first about the interaction between the security and the development issues that came out of the Sachs Report and the High-level Panel Report (HLPR); second, an additional dimension to what the SG brings, namely a greater focus on the rule of law and human rights; third, I'll go into more depth on some of the more institutional questions in the SG's report; and fourth, I will just talk very briefly about some of the points I think have been missed or misperceived or over-perceived in the initial reactions to the SG's report—which is part of the question of how we translate from words into political action, the topic of the panel itself.

I'll talk first about the interaction between the security and development issues in the SG's report; this is an issue that has been much debated these days in the UN and beyond. David already touched on it to a certain extent so I will just add some dimensions. I think it is important to say, as David noted, that the HLPR itself did put forward one of the more important aspects of this interaction in articulating the view that development is the essential precondition and the essential foundation of collective security for a range of reasons which David has touched upon.

In the initial reactions to the HLPR in New York and beyond, this was welcomed in some places and somewhat "unwelcomed" in other places, and I think it was in part because it was perceived to be saying that development is *only* important because it is a part of collective security, which isn't quite what the panel was saying. But nevertheless, there was a reaction to the HLP saying "look, development is more than just about collective security" and of course that's right—and one of the things the SG tried to do was to put these in a clear sense of perspective, saying in effect: development is important in its own right, even if it had nothing to do with security; the effort to help countries develop economically to combat poverty, to combat infectious disease is important in its own right. Just as the security issues are important in their own right, irrespective of whether they have any connection to development, combating terrorism, combating proliferation, or ending civil war, these too are issues that are important in their own right.

There is of course an interconnection between them, and I want to talk about that for a moment. And here, I want to be quite precise because there is a lot of rhetoric about these issues these days, there is a lot of research about them, some of it quite bad, and there is a lot of policy innovation around these, also some of it quite bad. You end up with quite a lot of phrases like "poverty causes terrorism" or "poverty is the root cause of terrorism," "poverty causes war" or "poverty is the root cause of war," "state failure causes terrorism" or "state failure causes proliferation"—there are a lot of these kinds of statements, and to our way of thinking, these statements have no basis in evidence, quite the contrary in some cases. Rather, what the HLPR did and the Sachs Report does, and what the SG's report does, is to try to understand the relationship between these issues in a much more complex way. The relationships between them are much more complex than just a simple causal pattern between poverty and terrorism, poverty and war. What we are really talking about is a risk relationship, the risk to development of the proliferation of small arms, the risk to development of the spread of civil war, the risk to development of the spread of terrorism or proliferation of weapons of mass destruction is quite significant. It is not a causal relationship but there is a huge risk relationship. It is self-evident in the risk to economic development of war—either within a country or even in the neighbouring region. What the HLPR was doing and the SG Report continues to do was point out that the relationship is also the other way around, which is often missed, certainly in security policy; that the collective security of our system does rely on combating poverty, does rely on combating infectious disease; that security even in narrow terms will not be achieved and will not be sustainable unless we can combat those ills, not only because it is for security reasons but *also* because it is for security reasons.

The connective tissue between the security issues and the development issues is the question of states—questions of state action and state capacity. This is the connection for all of what we are trying to do and it is here that we see the translation between rhetoric and action. Unless you get real action by states on the whole range of issues in front of us we will not see progress on these issues. This is not to say that states exist in isolation: states interact with civil society, states interact with the private sector, states exist in a complex social environment. But it is clear that the driving actor in the modern world and the driving actor in the contemporary period in terms of dealing with issues are states and *action* by states. But there is also a *capacity* question, and one of the themes that runs throughout these reports is the question of state capacity. If we are going to place increasing demands on states to deal with poverty issues, to deal with AIDS issues, to deal with security issues, if states are increasingly expected to cover a complex range of issues, they must have the necessary capacity to meet those challenges in a range of different spheres; and a major part of the development agenda and a major part of the reform agenda is about how we ensure that states have the adequate capacity to meet the challenges that confront them, and to participate fully in the international system.

And so in this sense, the SG's report is very much building on the two reports we heard earlier. The SG also then does something else, which is introducing an additional element which is not highlighted in the earlier reports; he emphasizes that if security and development are going to be sustained over time they must also rest on a foundation of the rule of law and of human rights: the rule of law both at the international and the national level and of human rights. And it's in fact the interaction between these three things, between security, development, and the rule of law and human rights that he sees as being embedded in the Charter, in the foundational principles of the United Nations and in this phrase from the very beginning of the Charter that stipulates what constitutes an effort towards larger freedom from which he took the title of his report.

In the section on rule of law he emphasizes three or four issues which I will quickly run through since they haven't come up in other discussions yet. The first is the need to strengthen the implementation of international humanitarian law, including adopting the norm of the "responsibility to protect"—and here I want to go into some details for a moment because this is a very controversial and a much debated issue. What he is saying is not that we need to develop new law. The law is quite good—if you look at the Geneva Convention, if you look at various protections under international conventions, if you look at the different statutory laws that we have, and if we look at Security Council (SC) precedence, there is lots of law. The problem is in implementation—and the call in the SG's report is to act on the legal provisions of the Geneva Convention, the legal provisions of the Genocide Convention, and the legal provisions of international humanitarian law. The "responsibility to protect" is a phrase, an emerging norm, but it is basically a call to implementation of existing commitments under international law, to protect civilians from the effects of war, first at the national level, if necessary through diplomatic and humanitarian. actions at the international level, and ultimately, if necessary, for military actions at the international level.

The second argument he is making here is about the International Criminal Court (ICC), in which he is essentially making a political argument about the vital importance of moving forward on the ICC in achieving full ratification and referring cases to the Court—and of course, just in the last days, we've seen now for the first time, the SC acting, albeit with some restrictions and some provisions, acting to accept that cases could be referred to the international court in the case of the Sudan.

The third point he is making in this section is to say that the UN as a whole, in the reform process, has to be strengthened in the area of human rights, that the capacity of the UN to help states and peoples improve their human rights is the vital part of the reform agenda. The HLPR pointed out that although human rights are one of the foundational principles and foundational purposes of the UN, the UN budget allocates precisely 2 percent of its overall resources to human rights activities within the system. The SG is reaffirming the point that there need to be significantly greater resources put into the human rights machinery of the United Nations.

The fourth point he is making in this section is about democracy, and he points out that in its various activities the United Nations is perhaps the organization in the world that has done most to promote democracy around the world through helping states develop their constitutions, by helping states with elections, by helping states in post-conflict reconstruction, and a host of other ways the United Nations contributes to the promotion and strengthening of democracy around the world.

So there is a security pillar in the March report, as well as a development pillar and a rule-of-law pillar. The fourth aspect of the SG's March report is to pull these down into the question of the institutions of the UN itself and the institutional reform agenda at the UN. Here there are basically four main arguments.

The first main argument is that if indeed security, development, and human rights are to be the priorities of the organization, this should be reflected in the intergovernmental machinery and intergovernmental structures. This translates to three specific recommendations. One, for reform of the SC, and Ed Luck can tell us this afternoon why that's a bad idea and others can contradict him; second, for reform of the United Nations Economic and Social Council (ECOSOC), and there will be several people in the room who can tell us why that is unachievable, and others why it is vital; and third, for reform of the Human Rights Commission, in fact of an upgrading of the Human Rights Commission to a human rights council either as a principle organ or a subbody of the general assembly, but in either case with different voting rules—and there will be lots of people in the room who will tell us why it's a completely terrible idea or why it is the most important thing we are talking about. These issues are of course very hotly debated, but the vision here is of three councils that match the three broad priorities and the founding principles of the organization.

The second argument, as David has already touched upon, is one of deep reform of the secretariat and there are lots and lots of details in it but they come down to two principles: first, increasing the managerial authority of the SG, to implement within priorities set by the members, to reallocate resources around priorities, to move resources and people to match priorities; and second, increasing the level of accountability on precisely that function; and here I want to spend a moment because given all the news reports about Oil-for-Food, etc., I think the word accountability requires some elaboration.

There are two types of accountability we need to discuss. The first is the kind of Oil-for-Food style of accountability—are we spending the money correctly, are people breaking the rules in terms of personnel, etc.—where there have to be strong systems of accountability in an accounting and performance management sense. Are we doing things properly in terms of how we manage budgets and personnel and related issues? But there is a second form of accountability, which is every bit as important if not more important, which is substantive accountability, i.e., is the SG implementing his mandates given to him by principal organs, doing what his bosses have told him to do? His bosses are the 191 member states who sit in the various councils and the General Assembly, who set the priorities of the organization. It's then up to him as Chief Administrative Officer to implement a number of these activities. Is he doing so in a way that matches the priorities set within the intergovernmental process? That is a substantive accountability, which quite frankly is missing in the administrative mechanisms of the advisory committee on administrative and budgetary questions. There is neither technical nor substantive accountability, nor does the SG have the managerial flexibility to perform properly within the range of tasks that he has. And so, all of the details really go to these two principles of increased managerial flexibility on the one hand and increased accountability on the other.

The third argument in this section is about the field. He makes the point—which of course everyone in the room knows fully well— that the UN at the field level has not always acted with quite the degree of coherence, quite the degree of coordination, quite the degree of concerted action that might be required in a number of circumstances, and he undertakes a set of commitments to do everything he can do to ensure that that occurs at the field level: that through the system of Special Representatives of the Secretary General (SRSGs), through the system of resident coordinators and through the system of humanitarian coordinators, there will be, to the extent it is possible in his authority, a single UN system on the ground that works in a concerted fashion. Obviously, these are issues that go to lots of complicated questions about governing boards and member states and donors, among others, but he is making a commitment to doing whatever he can do to ensure that on the ground the UN works in as coherent a way as possible.

The fourth major argument in the institutional section is the one that David has already mentioned, which is about regional organizations. David already laid out the issues here. I do think it's worth just highlighting again the character of this recommendation, which is recognizing—and this is not always done at the United Nations—that the UN does not exist in a vacuum. The United Nations is not the only international institution in the world; it's not the only solution to several of these problems. There is a slight tendency at the UN to find UN answers to every problem and I think the HLPR, the Sachs Report, and the SG's own report recognize that the UN does need to act within a context of both national and international bilateral and regional actors and actions and that there is an important partnership to be forged in a deeper sense than it has done before.

I want to talk quickly about the reactions in terms of things I think have been missed and things I think have been misinterpreted or over-interpreted.

The thing that I think has been missed is the question of prioritization. There is a long list of recommendations in an annex at the back of the report. What it somewhat missed is that in the analytical section of the report, the SG is suggesting priorities and they are reflected in the way these many recommendations are clustered in the various chapters. In the security section he says there are three basic priorities: taking urgent steps to prevent catastrophic terrorism; revitalizing the multilateral framework for managing disarmament; and proliferation and improvement of the UN's capacities to end civil wars through strengthening peacekeeping and strengthening peacebuilding.

On the development side, he is essentially setting up four broad priorities: achieving national strategies for MDG-based progress; a series of steps on the trade and financing for the development side to really make the resources for investment available; a series of steps on the environment side as have already been discussed; and setting out priorities in the rule of law, which I have already discussed.

Somehow I think this sense of prioritization has been lost in the reception of the report, and it may be that we didn't do a very good job in making clear that although there is a long list of issues there are some that are really priorities for action.

The last thing I want to do is to talk quickly about this idea of a package, touched on by both the Deputy SG and David. When the SG introduced the report, he did say that it is a package; people have interpreted this as meaning three things that he does not mean. He does not mean that it is take it or leave it, he does not mean that if one recommendation fails, they all fail, and he does not mean or expect that member states to whom this is addressed and who have a prerogative for decision making here are going to adopt these recommendations as they are, exactly as they have come—clearly not. What does he mean? He means first of all, as David has already said, that there are substantive interactions between these recommendations—you can't be serious about fighting poverty if you are not also serious about making progress towards ending civil wars. A state that is trying to develop and trying to combat poverty, that has to deal with the overflow of civil war in its borders, is not going to achieve the goals of combating poverty effectively. Ending civil war within the regional context is going to be a critical part of development within a given context. You cannot be serious about preventing biological terrorism without investing heavily in public health capacities around the world. You can't do it. So there are real and substantive interactions between the security and development and the human rights side of what's on the agenda. There are also, of course, political interactions.

The second thing that he means is that he hopes that member states will not cherry-pick and just say, "well these two or three things are easy so let's just work on them and we will drop the rest." He is hoping that member states will work on all of the issues across the range that the spectrum identified.

The third and most important thing that he means is if the macro goal here is a strong multilateral system that is grounded in a strong UN, progress needs to be made on all of these issues. A UN that is strong on security and isn't effective on development is not a strong UN. A UN that is strong on development and isn't contributing to human rights or countering terrorism isn't a strong UN. A strong UN is one that can meet the security challenges ahead of us and meet the development challenge ahead of us and make progress in the rule of law and human rights. This is the essential thing—a strong UN that comes out of the reform process will be one that makes progress in all of these areas.

FREEDOM FROM WANT

6 THE MONTERREY CONSENSUS
DEVELOPING THE POLICY INNOVATIONS

The International Conference on Finance for Development, hosted by Mexico at Monterrey in March 2002, came after nearly two decades of contention between the North and the South on macroeconomic issues in the UN and elsewhere.[1] Ever since President Ronald Reagan delivered his stark message at the North-South Summit held at Cancun, Mexico, in 1981, the developed world did not see global finance as a matter for North-South negotiation. The change came from three things—the consciousness of interdependence created by the financial crises of 1997–98, the strong support from several donor countries for the Millennium Development Goals (MDGs) and the concerns about alienation that came with the terrorist attacks of 11 September 2001. The Monterrey Consensus was reached because the UN managed to put together a credible process that used the political space created by these events.

Donor support for aid and other concessions has never rested on any deep commitment to the UN Charter. It was a product of strategic competition for influence in the Cold War, a spillover of colonial commitments in a few cases and, in some countries, an extension of welfare state values to the global sphere. That is why the bulk of aid and debt relief was delivered bilaterally rather than through the multilateral system. Even among the multilaterals, there was a strong preference for the international financial institutions (IFIs) whose voting structure gave donors effective control.

The classical motivations for development cooperation are not as relevant now. Colonial responsibilities are now largely forgotten, except perhaps in the European Union (EU)-Africa relationship, and the welfare state is in retreat even domestically. The Cold War is over, though the changing vectors of geo-strategic competition could stimulate the entry of new donors and new motivations. The heightened concern about terrorism after the 11 September 2001 attacks has also introduced a new interest in the links between development and security.

The United Nations played a major role in averting the threatened collapse of development cooperation in the early nineties with a series of path-breaking conferences. The core of the agreements reached in these conferences was captured in the MDGs,[2] which were crisp enough to cope with the attention deficit disorder on development issues in the media and the higher reaches of government. The impact of the conferences and the goals can be seen in the changing agenda of the G-7/8 meetings, in the growing willingness of the World Bank and the International Monetary Fund (IMF) to align themselves with the UN, and even in the Davos Forum. Thus the UN has helped to define a New Consensus on Development—a set of goals and policy approaches that all countries accept as a basis for international cooperation and national action. The outcome of the Monterrey Conference has to be seen as a part of this New Consensus.

Implementing the new consensus will require substantial changes in the way in which development cooperation is managed. In what follows, the tasks ahead are dealt with from the perspective of the Monterrey outcome, under five broad heads:

- Maintaining the agreement on goals
- Mobilizing international resources
- Managing the North-South partnership
- Securing coherence
- Reforming global economic governance

MAINTAINING THE AGREEMENT ON GOALS

The goals of development cooperation are now largely defined by the outcome of the UN conferences of the 1990s. These were essentially an attempt to provide a new type of rationale for development cooperation as a substitute for the old Cold War logic. They defined a substantive agenda for development, a shared understanding of the elements of good policy in a variety of areas like environmental management, poverty eradication, employment generation, social inclusion, education, health, gender equality, women's rights, and human settlements. They involved both national commitments and a promise of international support. In effect the case for aid, debt relief, and trade concessions now rested on the role they could play in attaining globally agreed ends.

The development goals enshrined in the Millennium Declaration are a product of these conferences. They were supplemented by the outcome of the Johannesburg summit on sustainable development.[3] They represent the most explicit global consensus on the goals of development that we have ever had. They provide a substantive basis for development cooperation shared not just by donors but by the recipients as well.

A large proportion of the developing country population now lives in countries that are not very aid dependent. Their commitment to the goals will depend on the extent to which these goals influence other areas of international cooperation like trade and investment.

In many ways these goals are a simplification of the task of development. They do not include enough about the investments in infrastructure, science and technology, and human capacity that are at the heart of development. They are thin on certain important concerns, for instance, those related to employment generation and work conditions or to gender equality. That is why they need to be kept under review so that any emerging consensus in any new area is quickly reflected in the development cooperation framework.

The goals are global. But the locus of action is at the national level. This requires a certain respect for national priorities. Poverty reduction will surely be accepted as a priority everywhere. But other concerns, like regional or group inequalities, self-reliance, or other national concerns may modulate it. Hence the principle that one size does not fit all should apply not just to means but also to ends.

Therefore the agreement of goals can only be maintained if we have a global political process that keeps them under review and that continues to look for new areas of consensus. In addition, a significant measure of flexibility has to be built into the process of implementation to allow for national variations, or, to put it more constructively, a national margin of interpretation.

MOBILIZING RESOURCES

The Monterrey Consensus was in part an attempt to strengthen the commitment to these goals by spelling out more clearly the expectations with regard to aid and the Conference itself witnessed major announcements of aid increases by the US and EU.

Aid levels have recovered from the decline during the nineties. According to the latest Development Assistance Committee (DAC) estimates, total aid from DAC members rose by 7 percent in real terms from 2001 to 2002 and by a further 5 percent in 2003. In nominal terms, official development assistance (ODA) rose by 18 percent from 2002 to US$69.0 billion in 2003. But about three quarters of the increase was due to the combined effects of inflation and the fall in the external value of the dollar. The ODA to gross national income (GNI) ratio rose to 0.25 percent in 2003, up from 0.23 percent in 2002 and 0.22 percent in 2001, but this is still well short of the average of 0.33 percent achieved in years 1980–92.

One of the most heartening features of the aid scene in recent years has been the growing commitment of European countries to the UN target of 0.7 percent. Denmark, Luxembourg, the Netherlands, Norway, and Sweden are still the only countries to meet or exceed this target. Four other countries have given a firm date to reach the 0.7 percent target: Ireland by 2007; Belgium and Finland by 2010; and France to reach 0.5 percent by 2007 and 0.7 percent by 2012. Spain has indicated it may reach 0.7 percent by 2012, and the United Kingdom that it may reach it by 2013. Several countries, which have not yet committed or indicated a target date for reaching 0.7 percent, have stated their intentions to raise their aid commitments. Canada intends to double its ODA between 2000 and 2010 and Switzerland has committed to an ODA/GNI ratio of 0.4 percent by 2010.

DAC has projected likely levels of aid for 2006 and 2010 on the basis of these stated intentions. According to their estimates, if these longer-term commitments are met, ODA will pass US$100 billion (at 2003 prices and exchange rates) by 2010.[4]

The direction of aid has also moved towards the countries most in need, and the bulk of the increase over the past four years is accounted for by the Least Developed Countries (LDCs). Sub-Saharan Africa accounted for about two-thirds of the rise. However, much of this was on account of debt forgiveness and emergency aid with just a modest real increase of US$0.6 billion in new money for development projects in the region.

The Millennium Project has estimated that the aid levels would have to double by 2006 and treble by 2015 if we are to meet what is needed for implementing the MDGs. This calculation assumes that the absolute level of aid for all activities not directly related to the MDGs would be more or less constant in absolute terms.[5]

The MDGs are not the only object of aid support. There are other worthy ends, like mitigating climate change or protecting biodiversity. There is also a need to recognize the need for aid to support plain, straightforward economic growth. Thus the UN Report reviewing the implementation of the Monterrey Consensus states, "It is also generally recognized that meeting these goals will deal merely with the symptoms of underdevelopment in the majority of member states. Additional financing will be required to allow them to achieve debt sustainability and the stable growth required to support permanent increases in per capita incomes."[6]

The requirements of aid are clearly larger than what is in sight, even with the heightened commitment that we have seen in recent years in many donor countries. The proposal for an International Finance Facility tries to meet this gap by front loading so that substantial sums can be mobilized immediately from the market against future aid commitments. If this is a more or less continuous process, it can help to raise the total amount available in the decade that we have to reach the MDGs. There are more ambitious proposals for raising resources by some form of global or globally agreed taxation. But they are unlikely to find favour any time soon.

Aid is a relatively small part of donor country budgets. Raising it substantially is not going to break the bank. The real challenge is to convince the public, their representatives in parliament, and treasuries that aid is a good investment in global development.

Debt relief is the other key plank in the Monterrey Consensus. External debt in developing countries stood at US$2.3 trillion at the end of 2002, compared with $1.4 trillion in 1990. External debt as a percentage of developing countries' GNI increased from 34 percent to 39 percent over the same period. Most of the increase was in middle-income countries, while the ratio fell slightly in low-income countries. From the perspective of the Millennium Goals the main concern is with the external debt of low-income countries which, at the end of 2002, stood at about $523 billion (of which nearly 80 percent was public and publicly guaranteed debt).[7]

To date, twenty-seven countries have qualified for debt relief of more than $55 billion under the Heavily Indebted Poor Countries (HIPC) Initiative. According to the World Bank this translates to their debt being cut, on average, by two thirds, and debt service to export ratios being reduced to an average of 10 percent. Yet, to place this in perspective, of the thirty-eight HIPC countries, only fifteen have satisfied all required actions to reach the completion point when the debt relief becomes irrevocable. Providing debt relief to the eleven remaining countries who have yet to qualify for HIPC is looming as a major challenge as the deadline for the entry into the program approaches.[8]

A key element of the HIPC Initiative was to redirect the funds that would have been used for debt service into poverty reduction programs such as education and health care. In African countries receiving debt relief under the initiative, poverty reduction spending has increased from 38.6 percent of government revenue in 1999 to 48.1 percent in 2001.[9]

Some lessons have been learned. The World Bank and the IMF are working on a framework to prevent lending to low-income countries from sparking a new debt crisis. The proposed framework, which has been discussed by the boards of the Bank and IMF, is a forward-looking approach that will involve conducting a more systemic analysis of borrowing country ability to repay debt before loans are approved. In countries where policies are sound, but the existing level of debt would mean new loans would jeopardize its debt sustainability, the framework calls for lending to be provided on more concessional terms or in the form of grants. One issue is the integration of the new debt-sustainability initiative into the International Development Association (IDA)-14 negotiations, which are currently underway with donor countries to the IDA. This may require a change in the current ratio of grants to loans in IDA and perhaps some scope for variation in the ratio across countries.[10]

The requirements for debt relief projected by the Millennium Project are very substantial—from $4 billion in 2002 to $13 billion in 2006. This is included in the estimates of additional ODA requirement mentioned above.[11]

Monterrey had much to say on the issue of middle-income country debt. The main demand here is for a mechanism that is more balanced between creditors and debtors and which is capable of bringing the private sector into any settlement. There is some progress in the use of collective action clauses. The Group of Twenty (G-20) countries has established a technical group to prepare a draft code in cooperation with private sector representatives. The intention of the code is to promote an early, voluntary dialogue between debtors and creditors on corrective policy and financial action to reduce the frequency and the severity of crises, to avoid disruptions, and to achieve more equitable burden-sharing in the process of crisis resolution.[12]

The third leg of the resource is the expansion of trade opportunities for poor countries. The main plank of this effort is the Doha Development Round, which nearly got derailed at Cancun. However, in July 2004, the negotiations were put back on track. The decision of the World Trade Organization (WTO) General Council of 1 August 2004 setting out frameworks for future negotiations carries forward negotiations in some key areas of the Doha work program. These areas include agriculture, market access for non-agricultural products, services, development issues, and trade facilitation. The decision also recognizes the development dimension of the Doha work program.[13]

The central principle of the WTO is that trade liberalization is good for development. However, WTO negotiations and domestic trade policy, particularly safeguard actions, are heavily influenced by large corporate interests. In this situation the benefits of trade liberalization are increasingly questioned by many non-governmental organizations. This sentiment will gain force if the outcome of the Doha Development Round does not bring tangible and timely results for developing countries, particularly the most poor amongst them.

There is in fact a more general problem of mandate creep in the world trade rules. Investment, intellectual property protection, and non-tradeable services (in some respects) have all been brought within the framework of trade rules. Principles like national treatment, non-discrimination between suppliers, and the irreversibility of liberalization are being applied to areas beyond the exchange of tradeable goods and services. In fact the meaning of the term "tradeable" is being extended to cover, for instance, the right of establishment to provide a service. Essentially the General Agreement on Tariffs and Trade (GATT) had negative rules about things governments could not do. The agreements covered by the WTO include provisions on what governments have to do, such as, for instance, pass laws to protect intellectual property on the lines specified in the Trade-related Aspects of Intellectual Property Rights (TRIPS) Agreement.

The emphasis on the Doha Round has to be balanced with the recognition that the deepening of regional trade agreements continues to be a central feature of trade integration for developing countries. Currently, approximately 40 percent of world trade takes place under regional trade agreements, and the share is expected to exceed 50 percent by 2005. Of the 285 regional trade agreements notified to WTO by 2003, 215 are in force today, and the number in force will exceed three hundred by 2007 if the sixty regional trade agreements currently under negotiation and the thirty at the proposal stage are successfully concluded. A major challenge for the global trading system is to work out how these regional agreements and the WTO framework can coexist.[14]

Mobilizing domestic resources is a part of the Monterrey Consensus and is central to the achievement of the MDGs. According to the assessment made by the UN many developing countries have made progress in the adoption and improved implementation of medium-term fiscal frameworks to improve fiscal accountability and transparency. This type of medium-term framework can provide the basis for multi-year aid commitments. Other measures that have been taken include the improvement of public debt profiles, the establishment of national commodity and fiscal stabilization funds, and reform and strengthening of the tax code and tax administration.

Remittances from expatriates are an important source of finance for many developing countries. In absolute terms they constitute a larger flow than ODA. Of course they do not go into the public budget and are not available directly for public purposes. However they do benefit many poor countries and tend to go to poorer households. The experience of the Indian State of Kerala shows how the flow of remittances can boost growth. A substantial part of these remittances flow through informal channels and the costs of remittance can be high. The importance of remittances is now widely recognized and several efforts are under way to reduce transaction costs. A policy measure that donor country governments could consider is to provide a tax set-off for remittances sent to poor developing countries.

MANAGING THE NORTH-SOUTH PARTNERSHIP

The New Development Consensus is essentially a North-South compact. The agreements on which it rests include an extensive enunciation of what good domestic policies should be in a variety of areas, including in the way political processes run. Good governance is supposed to be one side of a bargain where the other side is the promise of resources.

It must be recognized that the citizens of developing countries and their governments are as desirous of good governance as anyone else. According to the UN assessment, "Progress has been made in developing participatory political systems, but results have been more modest in enhancing transparency and accountability in Government, implementing the rule of law and the control of corruption."[15] At the global level the United Nations Convention against Corruption was adopted by the General Assembly in its resolution 58/4 and opened for signature at a high-level political signing conference, held in Merida, Mexico, in December 2003. This is a far-reaching convention that includes obligations on information exchange and on the return of looted money.

The link between governance and aid could shift the debate from partnership to conditionality, which has been a major source of contention in the development dialogue. Donors cannot manage without it, recipients feel constrained by it. Two quotations from the presidents who spoke at Monterrey typify this difference:

> "We must tie greater aid to political and legal and economic reform. And by insisting on reform we do the work of compassion." From the Statement by President George W. Bush of the USA at the International Conference on Financing for Development, Monterrey, Mexico, 22 March 2002.[16]

> "[Aid] should not be tied to conditions by donor countries, which is something we consider to be fundamental." From the statement by President Ricardo Lagos of Chile at the International Conference on Financing for Development, Monterrey, Mexico, 22 March 2002.[17]

There are some signs of change. The recent announcement by the United Kingdom's Department for International Development (DFID) that they now no longer believe in the virtues of conditionality is an example:

> We believe that [conditionality] is inappropriate and has proven to be ineffective for donors to impose policies on developing countries. Instead, we believe that successful aid relationships must be based on mutual commitment and dialogue, transparency and accountability.[18]

An expanded ODA program may well run into rough weather because of these differing beliefs on the role of prior conditionalities in the aid relationship. We need a constructive dialogue between donors and recipients. This will only be possible if we deconstruct this concept. This is attempted in the table below.

Table 1: Types of Conditionalities

	Non-economic	Economic
Not program related	Political Conditionality e.g., maintenance of democratic norms	Policy Conditionality e.g., promotion of free markets
Program related	Fiduciary Conditionality e.g., ensuring practices which minimize corruption	Performance Conditionality e.g., reaching agreed goals in the agreed time frame.

Source: Author

It is difficult to argue against the program-related conditionalities. If donors are investing in development then they surely have a right to assure themselves that the developmental results projected are reasonably probable. The main difficulty here is when donor aid organizations have excessively rigid or standardized views of what this requires in the program design. One size does not fit all. That is where the UK papers stress on country specificity and respect for national priorities and procedures is most welcome.

The real difficulty with the idea of conditionality is with those that are more general in nature and are not very directly related to the objects of expenditure in the supported program. The main justification for these is not really aid effectiveness but the politics of aid in the donor countries. The public and parliaments in donor countries want to be satisfied that their concepts of the good are being promoted by their aid administrations. This is an understandable concern. But it is akin to the belief that welfare payments to an individual should be conditional on his demonstrating loyalty to the ruling ideology. The donor countries have moved away from that long ago in their domestic arrangements and they must now move away from that in their international relations.

The logic for this shift is the same. The viability of democratic capitalism at the domestic level depended on the recognition that the unrequited transfers of welfare payments were necessary to sustain a functioning polity. This is now true at the international level. We have an international system that seeks to socialize states into a form of peaceable behaviour and practical cooperation. It does not always succeed, but its record so far is enough to justify continuing with the experiment. The central principle of this experiment is the sovereign equality of all states as the equality of individuals is at the national level. That is why this equality must be respected by avoiding any sense of imposition.

In a certain way the outcome of the UN Conferences and the Millennium Development Goals provide a solution. They are a global consensus of all states, not an imposition of one group of states on another. Requiring states to follow the goals and principles that they have agreed to in these conferences should be the broad political and policy conditionality asked for by donors. Even this, to the extent possible, should be left to regional peer review mechanisms, like the New Partnership for Africa's Development (NEPAD). Beyond that, the accountability in aid transactions would be strictly program-related. A shared understanding of conditionality, and its mirror image, partnership, is possible with the relaxation of attitudes on all sides and should be promoted through the dialogue processes suggested later in this paper.

SECURING COHERENCE

Trade, finance, and development policy have been brought together in the New Development Consensus. However, the forums, the actors, and the ideologies that guide action in these areas are very different. Coherence means that the countries, which accept a goal in one forum, will be prepared to be guided by it in other forums as well. So, for instance, the MDGs must become the starting point of negotiations in trade and finance forums. This does not always happen. The real difficulty is that the forums with a broad remit are not powerful and the forums that are powerful have a narrow remit.

Even amongst the forums that are powerful there is a problem of coherence. In the context of the Monterrey Consensus the link between trade and finance was much discussed. There is a Working Group on Trade, Debt and Finance (WGTDF) in the WTO. The agenda of the WGTDF consists of three issue clusters: the relationship between trade and finance; the relationship between trade and debt; and greater policy coherence between relevant institutions.

At the WGTDF session on coherence between the multilateral trading system and international financial institutions such as the World Bank and the IMF, Korea presented the case of bailing out its financial institutions as one example of lack of such coherence. According to Korea, IMF policies do allow government intervention for shoring up financial institutions in case of a crisis. However, when Korea—supported by the IMF—used about US$125 billion for strengthening its financial system, the EU initiated a WTO panel on the matter, claiming that this support amounted to an actionable subsidy.[19]

Brazil gave another example. Liberalization of the services sector was in most of the cases recommended or mandated by the IMF and the World Bank when granting structural loans. But this autonomous liberalization was not recognized in the WTO negotiations on services. Brazil saw this as an example of lack of coherence between the Bretton Woods institutions and the WTO.[20]

Developing countries in particular have highlighted the importance of examining the interlinkages between trade, debt, and finance in an effort to find sustainable solutions to these challenges within the context of the multilateral trading system. The continued availability of trade finance in a situation of financial crisis is an issue that cuts across the remit of the WTO and the IMF.

Institutional arrangements to secure coherence in global policy making are absolutely central to the implementation of the New Development Consensus. They must be at the heart of any substantial reform of global economic governance, a matter dealt with in the next section.

Coherence has to be secured at the domestic level with a broad concept of development cooperation. The main difficulty with the traditional understanding of development cooperation is that it limits greatly the range of policies in which the interests and concerns of developing countries are taken into account. In fact, this is often limited to the consideration of the aid budget, in debt rescheduling and in marginal trade concessions. Even in these areas, there is seldom any integration at the policy level. The measures taken are ad hoc and piecemeal. Thus the writ of the Development Cooperation Ministry often does not extend to trade concessions which the Trade Ministry may negotiate or even in debt management policies which the Finance ministries handle. There is a clear need to integrate at least the different dimensions of concessionality.

The integration that we need is not just for the concessional measures that fall within traditional notions of development cooperation. The reality is that the prospects facing developing countries are affected even more by the mainstream policies on trade, finance, agriculture, energy, immigration, etc. For the most part, these policies are determined by national interest as articulated by domestic lobbies. Development cooperation must encompass the systematic inclusion of the impact on developing countries in any analysis or international coordination of trade policies, fiscal and monetary policies, policies on agricultural subsidies, etc. The traditional concessionality would then become part of the broader package that includes changes in mainstream trade, finance and technology policies. This is the real goal of the Monterrey Consensus and the Doha Mandate.

REFORMING GLOBAL ECONOMIC GOVERNANCE

In the economic and social sphere, the global community works through a variety of multilateral processes for:

- the development of multilateral institutions which are entrusted with some measure of discretionary authority and predictable resources, and

- the codification of norms, standards, and principles that should be reflected in the laws, institutions, and policies of states.

Most of the multilateral institutions that deal with the first set of activities are outside the direct authority of UN processes and the Secretary General. On the other hand, a large number of the processes dealing with the second set of activities are within the United Nations. The main exceptions to this simple disjunction are the Monterrey issues of international finance and trade. Here both effective power and legislative capacity come together in the IMF (and related institutions) and the WTO. The SG's proposals for the role of the UN in development must be considered along with other proposals which address the reform of these institutions.[21] This is central to the agenda of many non-governmental organizations (NGOs).[22]

When it comes to maintaining the agreement on goals, the political space provided by the UN will continue to play a major role because of its universality and its capacity to deal with issues of norms and values. The shaping of a consensus on values, norms, and policy frameworks is something that the UN does which cannot be done with the same measure of broad acceptability by any other international institution. The basic reason for this is of course its universality, the broad mandate conferred by the Charter and the way in which its political processes create room for civil society. But in practice the major advances have come from the determined efforts of issue-oriented coalitions of states willing to pursue global interests. Such coalitions are most effective when they cut across the usual regional and interest groupings. The strength of the UN is that it has a political process that allows such coalitions to form and to work with the more organized interest groupings to achieve substantial advances.

The responsibility for the mobilization of resources and their efficient use will rest primarily with national governments. However the international arrangements for coordination like the IDA deputies meetings and DAC can be made less feudal, so that the recipient countries are not consulted as suppliants in an anteroom but as participants in decision making along with the donors.

At the country level, the growing importance of private finance and trade and the enmeshing of concessional and commercial resources suggests that we move away from donor-recipient stereotype to a source and destination country dialogue. This can be done by restructuring the usual annual Roundtables/Consultative Groups run by the Bank and

UNDP into a broad-based development forum, with an agenda anchored in the MDGs but shaped by national priorities of the developing country concerned. This is already happening in some cases and now needs to become the general rule.

The other two tracks for implementing the New Development Consensus—maintaining North-South partnership and securing coherence—will require more substantial changes in global economic governance.

The most important challenge is to give developing countries a substantially greater voice in the higher direction of the world economy. This requires both the integration of the large developing countries who have become major players in the global economy and better ways of reflecting the collective voice of developing countries in the IFIs and in finance and trade policy coordination.

A proposal which seeks to do this is the establishment of a small group summit of around twenty countries (G-20) which is representative and influential in directing the work of multilateral institutions. Such a G-20 cannot be a legislative or policy-making forum. That responsibility must rest with more universal bodies. The G-20 should be thought of as a committee of direction meant to ensure coherence across the work of multilateral bodies and to generate support and pressure for effective implementation of global commitments. How such a G-20 is constituted matters greatly for its perceived legitimacy as a coordinating forum. One proposal which addresses this suggests that the composition and the mandate of such a group should be the product of wide-ranging consultations conducted by a couple of countries which are seen to be disinterested because they rule themselves out from membership.[23]

A G-20 type process will not obviate the need to improve existing processes. The individual processes charged with the responsibility of overseeing each expression of values, norms, or principles must be better linked to one another. This has begun with the increasing attention being given to the idea of a coordinated follow-up to UN conferences, both in global and regional political processes and at the country level. It needs to be expanded to include the full range of the work of the UN in the economic and social sphere. It can form the basis for raising the value, credibility, and influence of ECOSOC in the eyes of the development community.

In his recent report on UN reform,[24] the Secretary General has stressed the role of ECOSOC as convenor and coordinator with a broad remit. He has proposed that it should become the high-level forum for monitoring progress towards the Millennium Goals and the extent to which development cooperation is being aligned with these goals. He has also recommended a strengthening of ECOSOC's role as a forum for discussing specific economic or disaster-related crises and for addressing the conflict-development link.

A more radical reform would be to merge the ministerial part of ECOSOC, the Development Committee and the International Monetary and Finance Committee of the IMF. Such a merger could provide the starting point for an Economic Security Council, which has been much discussed and was proposed by President Chirac at Monterrey. This *ménage à trois* will only work if there is some supervision by influential and representative countries at the highest political level, for instance through the G-20 type mechanism suggested above.

Effective implementation of what has been agreed to is the most urgent need. This requires a stronger connection between global policy-making and higher direction and the operational activities of the UN funds and programs, the World Bank and other multilateral aid agencies, and those of the bilateral donors. Each of these institutions is accountable for performance to its own governing body. Coherence requires that this be supplemented by some form of joint accountability to apex bodies like a strengthened ECOSOC or a new Economic Security Council or the G-20. The obligation to present a joint assessment will at least force these institutions to look at linkages between their activities and areas of responsibility.

Indeed one can go further and ask for at least a dialogue on performance between these institutions on the one hand and parliamentary representatives and NGOs on the other. The mechanism could be the joint parliamentary committees advocated by the Cardoso Panel.[25]

The effectiveness of implementation will depend not just on governments but also on the commitment of private entities that wield considerable influence in today's market economy. The Secretary General has launched the idea of a compact with the business community in order to strengthen the implementation of norms and goals agreed to in the UN process. The Turner donation has shown the possibility of tapping new resources. The sustainable development and environment processes have brought business into the policy dialogue. All three types of interaction need to be pursued with some vigour since this would raise the credibility of the UN not just in the world of business but also with governments.

The work of consensus building is by no means over. There is a continuing need to inject new analysis, insights and ideas into the political processes of the UN. Over the past decade the strongest creative impulse in the work of the UN has come from issue-oriented NGO movements. This has to be sustained. But the world of science and learning has not been as deeply involved in these processes. A systematic effort has to be made to connect with the academic world in order to inject new ideas and more rigorous analysis into the development dialogue. The Secretary General's announced intention of appointing a scientific adviser and a Council of Development Advisers are steps in the right direction.[26]

GETTING THERE

There is no shortage of policy initiatives and reform proposals. The real challenge is to get an agreement on priorities and a willingness to look beyond a limited tinkering within existing power structures and institutions, which is the most that has been achieved so far. To do this we need to understand and face up to what stands in the way of reform.

The most obvious problem is the elephant in the room. The United States possesses enormous military and economic power and finds that it can attain its national ends more easily through bilateral diplomacy and, on occasion, the unilateral exercise of power. They can find partners for such bilateral deals because a privileged relationship with the US seems to be the prudential goal of many governments.

The US has not opted out of the multilateral system. They remain very active in the UN, the WTO, and the Bretton Woods organizations. But their stance in negotiations is generally one of avoiding anything that would constrain national action and resisting any strengthening of international secretariats. One approach would be to secure stronger agreements without the US, as has happened with the Kyoto Protocol. The absence of the US would of course mean that the problem remains unresolved. However, a standard would be set which the US would have to accept at some stage since they cannot permanently stay out of such global agreements (or so we hope). The US would like to be seen as a good global player. The other countries have to ensure that the agreed definition or public understanding of what "good" means in this context is not constrained by US conservatism but reflects a broader consensus on what the world needs.

Developed countries other than the US seem more willing to accept multilateral obligations. A de facto multilateralization of aid is under way as more donors accept the UN goal of 0.7 percent, the MDGs as their goals, harmonize their procedures, work closely with the multilaterals and move to partnership as the basis of their relationship with developing countries.[27] Yet the processes of donor coordination remain restricted. This is where the developing country partners must insist on the next step which is a full involvement in aid coordination. Developed countries which are committed to strengthening multilateralism must go a little further. They must create space for a greater participation of developing countries in the Bretton Woods organizations, for instance in the positions on the Board. The present practice of reserving the leadership of the Bank and the Fund for the US and Europe also needs to be changed.

The developing countries are also changing. The larger ones are more conscious of their economic power. Many of them, with booming economies and rising reserves, are moving away from a suppliant mentality to a desire to play a role in global economic management. This was seen in the Cancun WTO meeting, which, even if it failed to secure agreement will be remembered as the time when the developing countries established that they have both negotiating capacity and strength in their unity.

A new coalition of the willing can be put together consisting of the developed and developing countries who have been in the vanguard of these changes in the aid and trade system to secure the more substantial changes that are needed in the UN and elsewhere. Other processes that engage global civil society and the private sector can add to the credibility and influence of this coalition. An agenda for reform is available. In order to get there those who are willing must not be held back by those who are not.

NOTES

1 *Financing for Development, Building on Monterrey* (New York: United Nations, 2002).
2 *United Nations Millennium Declaration*, General Assembly Document No. A/RES/55/2 (New York: United Nations, September 2000).
3 *Report of the World Summit on Sustainable Development*, Johannesburg, South Africa, 26 August–4 September 2002 (New York: United Nations, September 2002).

4 *Final Official Development Assistance (ODA) data for 2003 and simulation of ODA prospects for 2006, Development Assistance Committee* (OECD, February 2005).

5 *Investing in Development: A Practical Plan to Achieve the Millennium Development Goals: Overview,* UN Millennium Project 2005 (New York: United Nations Development Program, January 2005).

6 *Follow-up to and Implementation of the outcome of the International Conference on Financing for Development,* General Assembly Document No. A/59/270 (New York: United Nations, August 2004).

7 *Follow-up to and Implementation of the outcome of the International Conference on Financing for Development,* General Assembly Document No. A/59/270 (New York: United Nations, August 2004).

8 *Heavily Indebted Poor Countries (HIPC) Initiative—Statistical Update,* International Monetary Fund and International Development Association (Washington, DC: World Bank, April 2005).

9 *HIPC at a Glance,* at http://siteresources.worldbank.org/NEWS/resources/HIPC_glance.pdf, World Bank, n.d.

10 *Debt Sustainability in Low-Income Countries—Proposal for an Operational Framework and Policy Implications,* International Monetary Fund and International Development Association (Washington, DC: World Bank, February 2004).

11 *Investing in Development: A Practical Plan to Achieve the Millennium Development Goals: Overview,* UN Millennium Project 2005 (New York: United Nations Development Program, January 2005).

12 *Follow-up to and Implementation of the outcome of the International Conference on Financing for Development,* General Assembly Document No. A/59/270 (New York: United Nations, August 2004).

13 *Doha Work Program,* Decision Adopted by the General Council on 1 August 2004, WTO Document No. WT/L/579 (Geneva: World Trade Organization, August 2004).

14 *The Changing Landscape of RTAs* (Geneva: World Trade Organisation, November 2003).

15 *Follow-up to and Implementation of the outcome of the International Conference on Financing for Development,* General Assembly Document No. A/59/270 (New York: United Nations, August 2004).

16 *Financing for Development, Building on Monterrey* (New York: United Nations, 2002).

17 *Financing for Development, Building on Monterrey* (New York: United Nations, 2002).

18 *Partnerships for Poverty Reduction: Rethinking Conditionality,* A UK Policy Paper, Department for International Development (DFID), H.M.'s Treasury and Foreign and Commonwealth Office (London: Government of the United Kingdom, March 2005).

19 *The IMF's internal and global coherence,* SUNS-South-North Development Monitor, no.5260 at http://sunsonline.org, December 2002.

20 *Doha Round Briefing Series* 2, 10, The International Centre for Trade and Sustainable Development (ICTSD) and the International Institute for Sustainable Development (IISD), Geneva, August 2003.

21 *The Future of the WTO: Addressing Institutional Challenges in the New Millennium* (Geneva: World Trade Organisation, December 2004).

22 See material at www.brettonwoodsproject.org and at www.globalpolicy.org.

23 *Governing Globalisation-Globalising Governance*, Report of Track One on "New Approaches to Global Problem Solving" of the Helsinki Process on Globalisation and Democracy, (Helsinki, January 2005).

24 *In Larger Freedom: Towards Development, Security and Human Rights for All, Report of the Secretary General to the General Assembly*, General Assembly Document No.A/59/2005 (New York: United Nations, March 2005).

25 *We the Peoples: Civil Society, the United Nations and Global Governance: Report of the Panel of Eminent Persons on United Nations – Civil Society Relations*, (New York: United Nations June 2004).

26 *In Larger Freedom: Towards Development, Security and Human Rights for All, Report of the Secretary General to the General Assembly*, General Assembly Document No.A/59/2005 (New York: United Nations, March 2005).

27 *Paris Declaration on Aid Effectiveness*, Outcome of High-level forum cosponsored by AfDB, AsDB, EBRD, IADB, the OECD/DAC, the UN and the World Bank, Paris, March 2005.

JOHN W. McARTHUR

7 ENSURING ADEQUATE RESOURCES TO MEET THE MILLENNIUM DEVELOPMENT GOALS[1]

In 2005, the need for a dramatic global scale-up in official development assistance (ODA) is receiving rare public and political attention. Several high-level initiatives have recently put forward bold and practical policy recommendations for ODA, each stressing major increases as essential for both development and international peace and security. These recommendations have helped contribute to a frank global dialogue about the current state of international development assistance and the needs of the world's poorest people, many million of whom die needlessly every year due to their own extreme poverty and the ongoing shortfalls in ODA. This global dialogue has been given extra impetus in light of the tragic Asian tsunami of December 2004, the current G-8 process emphasizing support for Africa, and the September 2005 UN high-level summit progress since the Millennium Declaration, all of which have sharpened the focus on 2005 as the last chance for developed countries to decide whether they will ensure adequate ODA resources are available for the poorest countries to meet the Millennium Development Goals (MDGs) by 2015.

This short paper proceeds in five sections. The first outlines the major recent recommendations for ODA scale-up to achieve the MDGs. The second describes the links between these recommendations and the landmark framework for development cooperation established in the 2002 Monterrey Consensus. In light of the urgent need for incremental ODA commitments, the third section identifies policy and operational priorities for 2005. The fourth section describes the crucial role of the UN system in supporting ODA scale-up for the MDGs. The final section concludes.

MAJOR RECOMMENDATIONS FOR OFFICIAL
DEVELOPMENT ASSISTANCE

The Secretary General's High-level Panel on Threats, Challenges and Change was the first in the recent series of initiatives to give prominence to the need for major increases in ODA.[2] Stressing the inextricable link between development and security, the Panel asserted the centrality of achieving the MDGs, particularly through the implementation of MDG-based national development strategies in the poorest countries. The Panel recognized the need for greatly increased ODA to support those strategies, and therefore called for developed countries that have not already done so to achieve the long-standing target of 0.7 percent of gross national income (GNI) in ODA as an essential contribution to global peace and stability. Further emphasizing the core role of ODA in the pursuit of collective security, the Panel recommended that a clear commitment to the 0.7 percent target be considered as an important criterion for evaluating developed countries aspiring to permanent membership on the UN Security Council.

The second recent initiative was the UN Millennium Project, the Secretary General's independent advisory body mandated with recommending an action plan to achieve the MDGs, which presented its final recommendations in January 2005.[3] These recommendations include a detailed, needs-based approach to assessing the practical investments and policies required to achieve the MDGs, emphasizing that the international community should provide adequate finance and help support service delivery capacity through specific investments in human resources, infrastructure, and management systems. The UN Millennium Project also outlined how improved trade access is a critical contributor to the achievement of the MDGs, but that it is an essential complement to ODA rather than a substitute.

Assuming that developing countries themselves make tremendous strides to mobilize more domestic resources for poverty reduction over the coming decade, the UN Millennium Project found that ODA flows need to double in 2006 to $135 billion annually and continue to increase to $195 billion annually by 2015 (in constant 2003 dollars) just to meet the MDGs. The majority of these resources will need to be directed to supporting low-income countries' national development strategies, although many middle-income countries will also require assistance in direct ODA and through debt relief. Current commitments to scale up ODA by $30 billion annually by 2010 still fall $50 billion short of the level required for the MDGs that year. To meet the

MDGs along with other key development priorities, ODA will need to increase to 0.7 percent of developed countries' GNI by 2015. The UN Millennium Project therefore highlighted the urgency for developed countries to establish timetables to meet the agreed ODA target of 0.7 percent of GNI by 2015.

In March, the Commission for Africa chaired by UK Prime Minister Tony Blair outlined the need for an immediate ODA scale-up of $25 billion per year to Africa alone over the coming three to five years, followed by an additional $25 billion annually over the subsequent five years.[4] This level of need is highly consistent with the recommendations of the UN Millennium Project.[5] To help finance the required scale-up of ODA, the Commission for Africa also recommended the launch of an International Finance Facility to mobilize an immediate $50 billion of incremental development finance per year. These proposals are receiving serious international attention in the lead up to the July 2005 summit of G-8 leaders in Gleneagles, Scotland, which Prime Minister Blair will host.

Perhaps most importantly, March also saw the release of UN Secretary General's major report, *In Larger Freedom,* which set forth his recommendations for the actions needed to implement the vision of the Millennium Declaration, backed by a strengthened United Nations system.[6] Firmly reasserting the deep links between development and security, the Secretary General's recommendations on development policy and development assistance are bold and far-reaching, calling for major actions to translate the MDGs from loose aspirations to operational objectives. First and foremost, he calls for every developing country with extreme poverty to prepare and begin to implement, by no later than 2006, national poverty reduction strategies that are ambitious enough to achieve the MDGs. These strategies should be anchored in ten-year horizons and a needs-based approach to meeting each country's unique needs for human capital, infrastructure, environmental management, and private sector development. Second, his report calls for countries that produce those strategies to be provided with MDG-consistent international support, including adequate, predictable, and well-structured ODA. On a related note, the Secretary General also calls for a major increase in debt relief in order to ensure that MDG-based development assistance is not cancelled out by ongoing debt service payments back to donors.

To ensure developing countries are not impeded from achieving the MDGs due to a lack of resources, *In Larger Freedom* builds on the recommendations of the UN Millennium Project and the Commission for Africa by calling for all developed countries that have not already done so to reach the 0.7 percent ODA target by 2015, to meet an interim 0.5 percent target by no later than 2009, and to begin making significant increases no later than 2006. The report also focuses on the need for immediate availability of large-scale finance and rapid improvements in the quality of aid delivery. For the former, he calls for the launching of a full-scale International Finance Facility in 2005. For the latter, he calls for donor countries to agree, in advance of this September's high-level summit, on practical and measurable targets for linking support to countries' MDG-based national development strategies. Furthermore, the Secretary General supports the use of the 0.7 percent ODA target as a criterion for evaluating developed countries that are aspiring to international leadership through permanent membership on the UN Security Council.

ODA SCALE-UP IN THE FRAMEWORK OF THE MONTERREY CONSENSUS

The major reports described above have helped to focus the world's attention on the major and rapid increase in ODA that is required in order to achieve the MDGs and to support international peace and stability for the coming generation. They build on the landmark agreement established at the March 2002 Monterrey conference on Financing for Development, where developing and developed countries affirmed their framework for partnership, anchored in joint commitments to good governance for poverty reduction and to scaled-up assistance for developing countries that pursue such governance. This includes the important commitment in paragraph 42 that urges all "developed countries that have not done so to make concrete efforts towards the target of 0.7 per cent of gross national product (GNP) as ODA to developing countries."

Although increased development assistance is widely recognized as necessary for achieving the MDGs, it is certainly not sufficient for doing so. Countries wanting to reach the MDGs require sound national scale-up strategies underpinned by adequate resources and good governance practices. The latter includes a government's commitment to development and to implement effectively a major scale-up of public investments and services. In addition, good governance means upholding the rule of law through administrative and civil services and through legal and judicial institutions. It includes promoting human rights, particularly civil liberties and political freedom. It also includes sound economic choices, especially for macroeconomic policies and regulatory frameworks. And it surely includes transparent, participatory, and accountable decision-making processes underpinning a clear commitment to fight corruption. These many critical elements of governance serve as vital complements to the scaling-up of development assistance.

The term "poor governance" is often still used as a euphemism for corruption, despite the recent advances in research and measurement that have helped to clarify the variation in governance indicators across and within countries, capturing many of the dimensions of governance outlined above. The data show that some countries have high scores on an absolute scale while others, led by political reformers, score poorly, not because of their leaders' actions but because of entrenched corruption, possibly as a legacy of past regimes. Other countries are governed by corrupt rulers, while still others fall into violent conflict, making good governance difficult, if not impossible. The data also show that nearly every dimension of governance is highly correlated with income. This signifies a two-way relationship: good governance helps achieve higher income, and higher income supports better governance.

It is broadly accepted that better governance can lead to higher economic growth as a result of more efficient divisions of labour, more productive investments, lower transaction costs, and faster implementation of social and economic policies.[7] But it is not often properly understood that poorer countries with low levels of human capital are less able to ensure good governance, since this requires a well-functioning and adequately paid civil service, police force, and judiciary; proper information technology (e.g., for registration of property or transparency in procurement); equipment and training for a reliable police force; and many other outlays for proper public administration. Moreover, richer countries generally have more literate societies, with civil society organizations and media that are better able to act as watchdogs of public sector activities. Higher incomes also promote political participation and constraints on executive authority. The eminent economist Robert Barro, for example, has presented evidence to suggest that economic development supports the development of democratic political institutions.[8]

Furthermore, plenty of evidence shows that human capital is a fundamental predictor of economic growth and that rising human capital in turn seems to contribute to improved institutions. This is significant in the context of the 2005 pre-summit process since it suggests that external factors contributing to low human capital, such as endemic diseases (e.g., malaria) that lead to high child morbidity and mortality, can have an important adverse effect on the development of government institutions.[9] It also corroborates research by Xavier Salai-i-Martin and colleagues, who find that human capital and geography variables were among the main predictors of economic growth in the late twentieth century.[10]

The upshot is that while good governance can contribute to economic growth and bad economic governance can certainly impede growth, governance itself can be improved by investing in other factors such as education and health that support overall economic growth and human capital accumulation. This two-way causation is hugely important from the vantage point of the Millennium Development Goals. It underscores the significance of a broad-based strategy to meet the Goals, directly through good governance practices and indirectly through investments in human capital, public sector management, and infrastructure. It also highlights the point that on average a poor country is likely to have lower governance scores than a richer one, even if both governments have equally benevolent and committed political leadership. A proper assessment of a country's governance therefore requires not an absolute scale of measurement but a measurement in relation to other countries in a similar income group. Many government leaders in poor countries with weak governance systems are making heroic efforts at improvement, and those efforts need to be recognized and supported.

NEXT STEPS FOR DEVELOPMENT ASSISTANCE— IF THE MDGs ARE TO BE ACHIEVED

While a broad understanding of the links between development, governance, and ODA provides important guidance for the programming of resources for the MDGs, it should not distract from a more fundamental point for development assistance policy. In 2005, nearly five years after the establishment of the MDGs, the much-discussed relationship between governance and ODA remains divorced from the ground-level reality that even the *best* governed low-income countries are not receiving the ODA required to implement an MDG-based national strategy. Countries like Ghana and Tanzania, for example, are broadly recognized to have stable and transparent democratic processes and the ability to absorb and effectively invest much more ODA very quickly. Yet even they do not receive anywhere near the level or type of ODA required to achieve the MDGs. More broadly, no Poverty Reduction Strategy Paper is so far anchored in a ten-year scale-up framework to achieve the MDGs, backed by donor commitments to sufficient and predictable ODA over the period. In short, the international development system has not yet entrenched its MDG efforts in a practical model of success, so it is crucial that the first MDG-based national development strategies be adopted and implemented as quickly as possible in order to align broader development practice with the MDGs.

Moreover, without clear donor commitments to support national strategies that are bold enough to achieve the MDGs, there is little incentive and scope for a country, particularly a low-income country with major human resource constraints, to make the major national efforts required to draw up a ten-year scale-up framework for achieving the Goals. Many government leaders in developing countries are indeed frustrated by developed countries' repeated failures to follow through on development assistance pledges. These leaders are understandably hesitant to expose themselves to the political risk inherent in preparing an MDG-based strategy that sets their country up for disappointment again if the needed donor resources are not forthcoming. Nonetheless, in collaboration with the UN Millennium Project, several courageous and committed governments—including those in the Dominican Republic, Ethiopia, Kenya, Senegal, Tajikistan, and Yemen—have begun to prepare their own MDG-based poverty-reduction strategies over the past year and are planning to present them to their development partners over the coming months.

In these circumstances, the oft-suggested "chicken and egg" dilemma between donors and developing countries, whereby resources would be readily available if only more developing countries could demonstrate better governance, does not reflect the current reality. If the MDGs are to be achieved, the most fundamental constraint right now is financial, since donor governments have not yet even committed to making adequate resources *available* for the MDGs, even for the best-case countries. Credible commitments urgently need to be made for sufficient and reliable ODA volumes. Then, once the resources are committed, actual disbursements should be guided by appropriately rigorous standards of accountability and transparency.

TWO MAJOR ODA POLICY PRIORITIES FOR 2005

If the MDGs are to be achieved, two high-level policy priorities for ODA must be addressed well in advance of the September 2005 summit.

Adequate ODA Volumes Need to be Made Available

Timetables for reaching the 0.7 percent target are paramount, both to ensure adequate resources for the MDGs and because the 0.7 standard is perhaps the single greatest signal of developed countries' willingness to meet their own commitments to support development. That the MDGs are affordable within the 0.7 percent target, only adds to the urgency with which this target must be pursued. So far Denmark, Luxembourg, Netherlands, Norway, and Sweden have met the 0.7 percent target, while Belgium, Finland, France, Ireland, Spain, the United Kingdom, and most recently Germany have all set timetables for reaching 0.7 percent by 2015 (see Table 1). As the world's third largest economy, Germany gave fresh momentum to the global push for ODA to meet the MDGs with its April 2005 announcement to reach 0.7 percent by 2014. Nonetheless, given the short-term budgetary constraints in many developed countries, even if all existing ODA commitments are realized next year, a separate mechanism is required to mobilize the incremental $50 billion needed in 2006. A full-fledged International Finance Facility needs to be launched, as proposed by the United Kingdom, backed up by member countries' timetables for reaching the 0.7 percent target.

Scaled-up ODA Flows Must Be Programmed to Support on-the-Ground Investments through Developing Countries' MDG-Based National Strategies

Current ODA is generally not aligned with the investment priorities of developing countries, particularly low-income countries. The UN Millennium Project found that barely a fifth of bilateral development assistance and less than half of multilateral assistance finances direct investments for the MDGs. In scaling-up ODA, resources need to focus on supporting such direct investments, including through integrated, community-based scale-up initiatives and programs to train large numbers of new workers. The recent Paris High-level Forum on donor harmonization failed to confirm targets for donors to streamline their own development practices and to align them with the MDGs. However, the extension of their negotiation deadline to September 2005 still provides a window for developed countries to agree to support MDG-based national development strategies, anchored in 2015 commitment horizons, streamlined donor practices, and prioritization for budget support.

Table 1: Official Development Assistance among members of the
OECD Development Assistance Committee in 2003 and
Commitments to the 0.7 Target

Country	ODA as share of GNI in 2003 (%)	ODA in $US (billions)	Target year for achieving 0.7 target
Australia	0.25	1.2	No confirmed timetable
Austria	0.20	0.5	No confirmed timetable
Belgium	0.60	1.9	2010
Canada	0.24	2.0	No confirmed timetable
Denmark	0.84	1.7	Achieved
Finland	0.35	0.6	2010
France	0.41	7.3	2012
Germany	0.28	6.8	2014
Greece	0.21	0.4	No confirmed timetable
Ireland	0.39	0.5	2007
Italy	0.17	2.4	No confirmed timetable
Japan	0.20	8.8	No confirmed timetable
Luxembourg	0.81	0.2	Achieved
Netherlands	0.80	4.0	Achieved
New Zealand	0.23	0.2	No confirmed timetable
Norway	0.92	2.0	Achieved
Portugal	0.22	0.3	No confirmed timetable
Spain	0.23	2.0	2012
Sweden	0.79	2.4	Achieved
Switzerland	0.39	1.3	No confirmed timetable
United Kingdom	0.34	6.3	2013
United States	0.15	16.3	No confirmed timetable
Total ODA		**69.0**	

Source: Organisation for Economic Co-operation and Development, Development Assistance Committee, *Development Co-operation Report* (Paris: 2005)

TWO IMMEDIATE OPERATIONAL ODA PRIORITIES DURING 2005

In addition to these highest-level policy priorities, two urgent operational priorities are also essential for the first half of 2005. The clock is ticking as we approach the 2015 deadline, and the poorest countries certainly cannot wait for all international political negotiations to be resolved if they are to achieve the MDGs. Nor need they wait, since practical steps are at hand for immediate implementation in 2005.

Fast-track Support to Developing Countries as Soon as They Are Ready

Starting immediately, any country that puts forward a sound MDG-based poverty reduction strategy should be "fast-tracked" with commitments for adequate donor support. The first of such strategies could be presented as early as May 2005. These cases will be crucial for establishing a reference point for success. Fast-tracking should not be misunderstood to imply a focus only on short-term priorities. Instead, it implies initiating the ten-year scale-up process as soon as possible. Nor should fast-tracking imply an exclusive process in which countries receive support based on political or other arbitrary criteria. On the contrary, the only standards for fast-tracking should be: has the country prepared a sound MDG-based strategy that identifies an MDG financing gap, and can the country use ODA resources effectively to fill that gap?

Launch Some High-Impact "Quick Wins" as Soon as Possible

As outlined by the UN Millennium Project, it is possible for developing countries to start implementing some elements of a national MDG strategy immediately and to see dramatic results within three or fewer years. Although far from comprehensive, some "Quick Wins" could be jointly launched by developing and developed countries to bring vital gains in well-being to millions of people and start countries on the path to the Goals. With adequate resources, the Quick Wins include, but are not limited to:

- free mass distribution of long-lasting insecticide treated bednets and effective antimalaria medicines for all children in regions of malaria transmission by early 2008;
- ending user fees for primary schools and essential health services, compensated by increased donor aid as necessary, by no later than the end of 2006;
- successful completion of the "3 by 5" campaign to bring three million AIDS patients in developing countries onto antiretroviral treatment by the end of 2005;
- expansion of school meals programs to cover all children in hunger hotspots, using locally produced foods by no later than the end of 2006;
- a massive replenishment of soil nutrients for smallholder farmers on lands with nutrient-depleted soils, through free or subsidized distribution of chemical fertilizers and agroforestry, by no later than the end of 2006; and
- launching national campaigns to reduce violence against women, by no later than the end of 2006.

The Quick Wins need to be embedded in the context of longer-term national strategies to achieve the MDGs, but the world cannot afford to let another year go by without investing in these simple and proven strategies. Not only can huge numbers of lives be saved and improved but the successful early implementation of development programs backed by targeted donor assistance will also help to build longer-term support for ODA in developed countries not yet committed to 0.7 percent timetables.

PRACTICAL ROLES FOR THE UN SYSTEM

In 2005 and beyond, the UN system will need to play a central role in supporting the scale-up of ODA and advancing the broader MDG agenda. In particular, the UN system will need to emphasize its respective functions as a forum for intergovernmental processes, as an operational network of leading technical organizations, and as an evaluative body that monitors and promotes progress towards agreed international standards.

Convening Intergovernmental Processes

The UN is the forum in which member states will negotiate the outcomes for the September 2005 summit. It is here that delegates will need to translate the substantive links between development and security into clear policy agreements. They will undoubtedly need to remind each other of the existing 0.7 percent target and the need for timetables to achieve it. Member states can also negotiate specific timetables and targets for donor governments and their partner countries to harmonize procedures and practices around MDG-based national strategies.

Providing Technical Support

On the operational side of the UN, the specialized agencies, programs, and funds have a core role to play in providing technical support to countries developing and implementing MDG-based poverty reduction strategies. In several areas, UN organizations are the leading international repositories of technical expertise so they will need to organize themselves to play the most constructive role possible when countries require help in preparing or implementing MDG-based national scale-up programs. At the same time, individual agencies, programs, and funds can also take leading roles in coordinating the global partnerships required to launch several Quick Wins. The World Food Program, for instance, could help put together the coalition that will manage the Quick Win for locally produced school meals. UNICEF and the World Bank could help to lead the effort to end primary school fees in low-income countries. The World Health Organization (WHO) could work with the Global Fund to Fight AIDS, Tuberculosis and Malaria and other key partners to ensure full coverage of effective anti-malarial medicines within three years.

Promoting International Standards

The UN already coordinates the global effort to evaluate and report on MDG progress around the world. This includes both a cross-country data monitoring effort and support for national reports aiming to capture more nuanced ground-level realities. Moving forward, the UN will need to link this reporting role to the promotion of national policy standards that are consistent with the MDGs. It is common, for example, for developing countries to lag in particular sectors, due either to resource constraints or to general policy neglect. Education strategies are often given funding priority over health when countries feel they cannot afford to invest in both at scale. Health indicators and outcomes suffer tremendously as a result. Meanwhile, many countries have systematically neglected policies for the environment and maternal health, mainly due to oversight. In such instances, and particularly as more ODA is made available for the MDGs, the uniquely respected country-level voice of the UN is crucial for working with national governments to advocate a broad and fully integrated policy approach that gives adequate emphasis to all sectors and areas within sectors. In advancing this integrated approach, the UN will be able to advance the MDGs, not just as indicators but as agreed minimum standards for framing development policy.

CONCLUSION

In 2005, the UN member states will take many important decisions that lay the foundation for international policy-making over at least the coming generation. None of these decisions could be more important than those regarding official development assistance for the MDGs. On current trajectory, there is little question that millions of the world's poorest people will die needlessly over the coming decade due to developed countries' lack of follow-through to provide adequate ODA.

Fortunately, developed country leaders have the opportunity in the coming months to change that trajectory. Most importantly, they can decide to follow through on their Monterrey commitments by establishing clear timetables to reach the long-standing 0.7 percent ODA target by 2015. They can commit to centring their ODA support on developing countries' own MDG-based strategies, starting as soon as those strategies are ready. And they can commit to supporting immediate Quick Win actions to save large numbers of lives without delay. In all of these areas, the UN must play a central role by helping to forge intergovernmental agreement, by providing the technical leadership required to achieve the MDGs, and by promoting the standards that developing countries can adopt as they begin to operationalize the Goals.

These decisions and actions are all feasible in 2005. If taken, they will mark a long-awaited breakthrough for international development policy and at last make possible the achievement of the MDGs. More importantly, they will help turn the tide against the world's most extreme forms of poverty, saving and improving many millions of lives in the process.

NOTES

1 Section 2 of this paper draws directly from chapter 7 of the UN Millennium Project's final report, *Investing in Development: A Practical Plan to Achieve the Millennium Development Goals* (New York: Earthscan, 2005).

2 United Nations, *A More Secure World: Our Shared Responsibility*, Report of the Secretary General's High-level Panel on Threats, Challenges, and Change (New York: United Nations, 2004).

3 UN Millennium Project, *Investing in Development: A Practical Plan to Achieve the Millennium Development Goals* (New York: Earthscan, 2005).

4 Commission for Africa, *Our Common Interest: Report of the Commission for Africa* (London: 2005).

5 Although the UN Millennium Project did not publish regional ODA needs in its final reports, the Project's underlying analysis, when evaluated on a region-by-region basis, shows that ODA needs are highly consistent with those estimated by the Commission for Africa.

6 United Nations, *In Larger Freedom: Towards Development, Security, and Human Rights for All*, Report of the Secretary General, A/59/2005 (New York: United Nations, 2005).

7 P. Mauro, "Corruption and Growth," *The Quarterly Journal of Economics* 110, 3 (1995): 681–712.

8 R. J. Barro, "Determinants of Democracy," *Journal of Political Economy* 107, 6 (1999): S158–83.

9 E. Glaeser, R. LaPorta, F. Lopez-de-Silanes, and A. Shleifer, "Do Institutions Cause Growth?" *Journal of Economic Growth* 9, 3 (2004): 271–303.

10 X. Sala-i-Martin, G. Doppelhofer, and R. Miller. "Determinants of Long-Term Growth: A Bayesian Averaging of Classical Estimates (BACE) Approach," *American Economic Review* 94, 4 (2004): 813–35.

FREEDOM FROM FEAR

8 WMD AND TERRORISM
CAN THE UN HELP TO KEEP THE GENIE IN THE BOTTLE?

On 13 April 2005, the United Nations General Assembly adopted by consensus an international treaty against nuclear terrorism.[1] Thus the Nuclear Terrorism Convention (NTC) will open for signature on 14 September 2005 and enter into force after twenty-two states ratify it. This step coming after seven years of negotiations and less than a month after the report of the Secretary General, *In Larger Freedom: Towards Development, Security and Human Rights for All,* issued on 21 March, is a happy augury for more decisive action by the UN to ensure that nuclear, biological, and chemical weapons, i.e., weapons of mass destruction (WMD), do not fall into the hands of terrorists.

The Secretary General's report contains a warning of the dangers of "catastrophic terrorism." This warning has been repeated with increasing levels of urgency in the policy making community especially after the events of 11 September 2001, since it is well known that groups such as Al Qaeda have had plans to acquire WMD. The report recommends measures to be adopted by member states, such as the recommendation that negotiations for an international convention for the suppression of nuclear terrorism be completed. However no other specific tasks or reforms of the United Nations (UN) have been recommended to ensure that the UN is able to play a significant and effective role in the prevention of WMD terrorism.

The High-level Panel, appointed by the UN Secretary General to assess current threats to international peace and security, came out with a report that has addressed the issues of WMD and terrorism separately.[2] While warning about WMD proliferation, making a specific identification of the threat of WMD terrorism, and recommending that the UN and specialized agencies take preventive action, the link between WMD and terrorism has been clearly established. Paragraphs 135 to 138 make the link explicitly. Paragraph 135 proposes urgent "short-term action" to defend against the "possible terrorist use" of WMD through the consolidating, securing and, when possible, eliminating of hazardous materials and implementing effective export controls. The Global Threat Reduction Initiative is welcomed by the Panel but the timeline for its implementation is recommended for halving to five years. The Security Council, acting under resolution 1540, is urged to provide states with model legislation for action on WMD materials and the establishment of minimum standards by 2006 and a permanent liaison between the committee implementing Security Council resolution 1540 and the International Atomic Energy Agency (IAEA), Organization for the Prohibition of Chemical Weapons (OPCW) and the Nuclear Suppliers Group (NSG). In dealing with a definition of terrorism, the problem of WMD terrorism is clearly kept in mind. While all these are laudable recommendations they do not by themselves ensure that the UN will be at the centre of global efforts to counter the threat of WMD terrorism nor that it will be the most effective body in this task. More will have to be done to identify the actual threat and keep it under review and devise defences against these threats. To do that we must review what the UN has said and done in the past.

Speaking at the UN General Assembly on 1 October 2001, Secretary General Kofi Annan said, "It is hard to imagine how the tragedy of 11 September could have been worse. Yet, the truth is that a single attack involving a nuclear or biological weapon could have killed millions. While the world was unable to prevent the 11 September attacks, there is much we can do to help prevent future terrorist acts carried out with weapons of mass destruction." He went on to propose strengthening the global norms against the use or proliferation of WMD by redoubling efforts to ensure the universality, verification, and full implementation of key treaties relating to WMD; promoting cooperation among international organizations dealing with these weapons; tightening national legislation over exports of goods and technologies needed to manufacture WMD and their means of delivery; and developing new efforts to criminalize the acquisition or use of WMD by non-state groups.

More recently, on 10 March 2005, Secretary General Annan in his "five Ds" speech in Madrid said, "Nuclear terrorism is still often treated as science fiction….That such an attack has not yet happened is not an excuse for complacency. Rather it gives us a last chance to take effective preventive action." He went on to identify biological terrorism as a threat against which state capacity had to be built up with local health systems at the front line.

In the almost three-and-a-half years between the two statements, the UN has acted to prevent WMD terrorism as the global appreciation of the extent of the problem increased. It is useful to describe this action briefly as well as the current estimates of the threat of WMD terrorism before we identify ways and means for the UN to act more effectively.

WHAT THE UN HAS DONE SO FAR

The threat of WMD terrorism predated the terrorist attacks in the United States on 11 September 2001. Events such as the 1995 use of sarin gas in the Tokyo subway had already alerted the world to the possibility of WMD terrorism, which several instances of the theft of WMD material and the likelihood of WMD technology experts being lured by non-state actors only served to underline. Many experts in the field had already written extensively on the subject and individual countries had taken measures to prevent the threat from materializing. The US Nunn-Lugar legislation, which grew into the Co-operative Threat Reduction program, was one example where US concerns about the safe custody of nuclear materials and the future of the nuclear scientists in the countries of the former USSR were translated into a practical program of action which was later supported by the G-8. The UN's Department for Disarmament Affairs kept these developments under regular review. The adoption of Security Council resolution 1373 (2001) provided a broad framework within which the UN could now act under Chapter VII. Strengthening the capacity of member states was a priority and with the Counter Terrorism Committee (CTC) in place and headed in its first few years by the very effective UK Permanent Representative, Sir Jeremy Greenstock, the prevention of WMD terrorism was also addressed. Revitalized through Security Council Resolution 1566 (2004), the CTC established an Executive Directorate to enhance its co-ordinating function in implementing resolution 1373 and in capacity-building.

In August 2002 the Secretary General published the report of his Policy Working Group, which made several recommendations including the biennial publication of a report on WMD terrorism;[3] development of the technical capabilities of the IAEA, the OPCW, and the WHO to provide assistance to states in the event of the threat or use of WMD; arrangements to develop and maintain adequate civil defence capabilities through the same organizations; the creation of codes of conduct for scientists aimed at preventing their involvement in terrorist activities and the restriction of public access to expertise on the development, production, and stockpiling and use of WMD. There is no indication that any of the recommendations have been pursued energetically although an enhanced level of inter-agency coordination has certainly begun.

The Security Council has undoubtedly been the engine room where much of the action on combating terrorism in general and WMD terrorism in particular has been taken. The CTC has been crucial in this, but beyond making assessments of state capabilities to prevent and respond to WMD terrorism no measures had been initiated within the UN system to enhance the capacity of the organization to respond to the challenge. The major achievement which changed this has, of course, been the adoption by the Security Council on 28 April 2004, of resolution 1540 under Chapter VII of the Charter as a comprehensive ban on support to non-state actors in the development or acquisition of WMD. The resolution is a call to all states to adopt measures for the safe custody of WMD materials and more proactive measures to prevent proliferation of WMD. Most importantly a Committee of the Security Council was established to report on the implementation of the resolution and national control lists were requested from member states. This resolution greatly empowers the UN to act decisively on WMD terrorism and provides a mechanism to coordinate action within the UN system and with member states. It is too early to assess how effective the resolution and the Committee established to oversee its implementation has been.

THE PARAMETERS OF THE PROBLEM

The need for a pragmatic balance between panic-driven reactions and smug complacency is self-evident. Deconstructing WMD terrorism is also vital because the nature of the weapons grouped under WMD varies greatly and the threat assessment of terrorist acquisition and use of these weapons also differs. All three categories of weapons have the potential of inflicting a scale of death and destruction higher and more long-lasting than conventional weapons as well as the capacity to terrify and coerce populations. Conflating nuclear, biological, and chemical weapons as WMD is misleading because of the distinct physical and political effects of these weapons. Some experts add radiological weapons as a separate WMD category, despite its close link to the nuclear weapon category.

Nuclear weapons are the greatest threat because of the lethality of the weapons, their long-lasting effects on the environment, and the danger that a nuclear exchange would lead to the devastation of large areas of the world. The easy availability of the technology on how to manufacture nuclear weapons is well-known, so much so that experts have concluded that any intelligent student of physics could acquire the knowledge of how to make a nuclear weapon. The access to nuclear weapon material, whether enriched uranium (HEU) or plutonium, in sufficient quantity to make a nuclear bomb, is also well-documented. HEU is more sought-after because of the ease of making a gun-type device. The startling revelations of the nuclear bazaar run by the Pakistani scientist Dr. A.Q. Khan and his network have proved how widespread the illicit trade in nuclear materials has been. And yet experts doubt the capacity of non-state actors to organize the elaborate infrastructure necessary to manufacture nuclear weapons in a clandestine fashion, undetected by the national technical means of major states through satellite surveillance and through intelligence agencies. This may still be possible either in a failed state or in a state which permits this kind of activity unless inspection under IAEA safeguards recently enhanced by the Additional Protocol is taking place. This conclusion refers to nuclear weapons similar to what states require, whereas non-state actors are more likely to seek more crude and improvised nuclear devices (IND). The absence of an international norm banning nuclear weapons heightens the risk of nuclear terrorism. Nuclear terrorism can also take the form of a terrorist seizure of a nuclear weapon that has been made in a nuclear weapon state or the bombing of a nuclear installation as a deliberate attempt to disperse radioactive material.

Biological weapons are the next greatest threat because pathogens or toxins can be easily made in a small area and if spread in sufficient quantities could cause widespread deaths causing alarm and panic. Biological weapons are banned by the 1972 Biological Weapons Convention (BWC), but the absence of effective verification measures and an organization to implement the BWC are serious inadequacies. The developments in biotechnology, easy availability of materials needed for biological weapons, and the possibility of their manufacture being undetected has heightened the fears of this category of WMD terrorism more than any other. The yet undetected perpetrator of the anthrax letters in Washington, DC, in late 2001 and the earlier 1984 contamination of salad bars in Oregon with the non-lethal salmonella pathogen are examples of how biological weapons can be used to cause panic. Biological weapons can not only be used against humans but also against crops and livestock adding to social disruption. Some micro-organisms can attack physical infrastructure by degrading plastics. Biological agents—bacterial organisms, viruses, or toxins—have to be weaponized to cause harm. They have also, as with nuclear weapons, to be delivered. And yet the psychological consequences of the threat or actual use of biological weapons is great. Most experts believe that terrorist use of biological weapons is more likely than nuclear weapons despite problems in growing bulk quantities of biological seed stock, weaponization and delivery.

Chemical weapons have been banned through the Chemical Weapons Convention (CWC), which entered into force in 1997 and has effective verification measures implemented by the OPCW in The Hague. This is an effective bulwark against the likelihood of terrorists using this category of WMD. Effective control and supervision of supply of precursors of chemical weapons, arrangements for assistance in the event of a threat or use of chemical weapons and provisions for no-notice inspections have built confidence among state parties in the CWC. Nevertheless the CWC is not universal and has 167 parties. Moreover chemical weapon stocks have still to be destroyed in many countries and their safe custody is doubtful. The extent of damage that can be caused by chemical weapons is regarded as less than by nuclear or biological weapons.

Radiological weapons have been identified as a more likely weapon to be used by terrorists. Simple high-explosive bombs can be used to disperse radioactive material such as the cobalt used in industrial plants. This device, or "dirty bomb," would be difficult to handle safely, but it could still cause widespread deaths and damage, spreading panic. The scale of death and destruction would still be much less since the radiation would not spread beyond the blast area. The reports of thefts of nuclear material make this form of terrorism likely.

Finally, WMD terrorism would require delivery vehicles in the form of missiles or airplanes to be really effective. However, IND could be assembled on site and/or delivered in a truck or van. Small quantities can of course be smuggled in through airports and seaports or across borders. Increased surveillance, through improved technology, minimizes the risk but does not eliminate it.

CONSTRUCTING UN BARRIERS AGAINST WMD TERRORISM

There is no doubt that the international community regards WMD terrorism as a threat to international peace and security. It follows that the UN must be at the centre of all efforts to combat this danger. It is a danger that can be controlled through effective cooperation by all member states if cooperative security is to be a meaningful concept. Prevention of the danger of WMD terrorism is obviously better through peaceful means than through pre-emptive action of a military nature. Military action to destroy suspected WMD-capable sites could carry greater risks to life and can create the very panic that one seeks to avoid.

A number of proposals have been made, both within the existing treaty regimes and outside, for the international control of WMD proliferation in general—such as the Proliferation Security Initiative (PSI)—which will of course reduce the danger of WMD terrorism. Some are specific to the type of WMD involved. For example the latest report of the Carnegie Endowment for International Peace on "Universal Compliance - A Strategy for Nuclear Security" recommends six obligations:

- making non-proliferation irreversible by tightening the controls on the production of fissile material and rules for withdrawal from the NPT;
- devaluing the political and military currency of nuclear weapons;
- securing all nuclear materials by adopting more robust standards;
- stopping Illegal Transfers with national legislation to implement UNSC resolution 1540 etc.;
- committing to conflict resolution since non-proliferation measures alone are not enough; and
- solving the problem of the three states with a nuclear capability outside the NPT by persuading India, Israel, and Pakistan to accept the same non-proliferation obligations of the nuclear weapon states within the NPT.

The above recommendations, *mutatis mutandis*, could apply to the other categories of WMD. They could also be adopted with the active assistance of the UN and/or the respective treaty bodies involved. The Madrid Agenda of 11 March 2005 also contains specific recommendations on WMD terrorism.

It is logical that the UN, as the only universal body legitimately empowered by its 191 member states to maintain international peace and security, should be at the forefront of the global effort to combat the threat of WMD terrorism as an important component of the campaign against terrorism. This task has to be undertaken in a coherent manner without duplication of other efforts and without overlap with the work done by existing treaty regimes, multilateral groups, and Interpol.

The definition of terrorism proposed by the High-level Panel and fully endorsed by the UN Secretary General in his report has important consequences for states apart from the (now fulfilled) obligation to conclude the protracted negotiation of a convention to prevent nuclear terrorism. The reference to the Geneva Convention implies adherence to the humanitarian principles of war. The International Court of Justice's 1996 landmark Advisory Opinion ruled that the use of nuclear weapons was generally contrary to the existing humanitarian principles of war. Thus the proposed definition effectively places a legal obstacle against state use of all WMD including nuclear weapons. While this would be logical for state parties to the BWC and the CWC it would universalize the actual ban on the use of biological weapons and chemical weapons to non-state parties as well. More importantly it would apply to nuclear weapons where there is no legal ban on the actual use of these weapons. Thus states whose defence doctrines are predicated on the use of nuclear weapons either as a weapon of last resort or for pre-emptive use even as "bunker busters" would feel restrained by this definition and may be reluctant to accept it in its present form. A comprehensive convention on terrorism is certainly desirable in the ban on WMD terrorism but doing so without also addressing the larger issue of the elimination of all WMD, whether by states or non-state actors, would cause great difficulty. A universal norm needs to be established if WMD possession by non-state actors is to be effective. To argue that possession by some states is permissible would be difficult to sustain. Nor is it logical to regard the proliferation of WMD and their use by non-state actors as a threat to international peace and security while nuclear weapon possession by some states continues.

There are, however, many other proposals to prevent WMD terrorism which can and must be implemented. They include the implementation of the recommendations of the UN's Policy Working Group referred to earlier. The strengthening of the NPT regime has been proposed by many through a number of measures to be implemented especially by the IAEA in respect of its responsibilities for safeguarding nuclear material and making the transition from peaceful uses of nuclear energy to nuclear weapon production more difficult.

The existing export controls of nuclear and chemical material are implemented by the Nuclear Suppliers Group and the Australia Group outside the UN. They are viewed as discriminatory and a dialogue within the UN of suppliers and recipient states may help to increase understanding regarding the paramount need to prevent WMD terrorism through tighter export controls. At the same time, in line with the Trilateral Initiative, the IAEA, Russia, and the US should place more nuclear materials under controls. This initiative could be extended to other nuclear weapon states.

A series of other proposals have been made for the UN to establish stronger barriers against WMD terrorism. They include those that have already been mentioned in the body of this paper, plus:

- the strengthening of the capacity to verify the leakage of materials and technology such as through the institutionalization of the existing expertise in UNMOVIC as far as biological weapons and missiles are concerned;
- the mandatory requirement for Non-Proliferation Treaty (NPT) state parties of signing and ratifying the IAEA's Additional Protocol in order to qualify for supplies for the peaceful uses of nuclear energy;
- The framing of a code of ethics for scientists in the defence sectors and in research establishments ensuring the non-transfer of knowledge to non-state actors.
- strengthening the IAEA's Convention on the Physical Protection of Nuclear Materials;
- providing all member states with stakeholder status by creating a separate Commission on Terrorism under ECOSOC or the UN General Assembly (UNGA), using Article 68 of the Charter, where WMD terrorism can be discussed. Sharing of intelligence will also be necessary; and
- criminalizing the illegal possession of WMD material through national legislation.

This is by no means an exhaustive list. Accountability by member states is finally the only means of ensuring that non-state actors are prevented from using WMD for terrorist purposes.

NOTES

1 United Nations General Assembly Document No. A/59/766 (New York: United Nations, 13 April 2005).

2 United Nations, *A More Secure World: Our Shared Responsibility*, Report of the Secretary General's High-level Panel on Threats, Challenges, and Change (New York: United Nations, 2004).

3 United Nations General Assembly Document No. A/57/273 (New York: United Nations, August 2002).

TOM FARER

9 LEGAL AND LEGITIMATE USE OF FORCE UNDER THE UN CHARTER

A CRITICAL ANALYSIS OF THE REPORT OF THE HIGH-LEVEL PANEL

INTRODUCTION

Contemporary conflict over the meaning and the legal status of use-of-force constraints in the Charter and the problématique of the original understanding

Within the past few years, a number of international lawyers, mostly from the United States, have argued that Charter norms purporting to regulate the use of force have become so inconsistent with state practice that they can no longer be deemed legally binding.[1] These Charter skeptics (as I call them) do not appear to be claiming that practice has modified the original interpretation of those norms. Their claim, rather, is that practice has demonstrated the collapse of the interstate consensus, assuming a real one ever existed, necessary to sustain the Charter normative scheme.

Precisely what legal conclusions follow from this notionally empirical observation is unclear. One possible conclusion is that the question of when a state can employ force has become entirely political in character. Hence, it is possible to condemn particular uses of force only on the grounds that they are immoral or imprudent. An alternative possibility is that certain broad legal prohibitions persist, in particular the preclusion of force where its only justification is to impose the value system of the aggressor or to increase its wealth and power. Or, to put the test in slightly different terms, the use of force is legal whenever it can be plausibly characterized as a good-faith defence of vital interests of the aggressor threatened by its target or in defence of Charter values like basic human rights.

Are these chroniclers of the supposed demise of the use-of-force regime telling a true story? If so, where can we go from here, and how do we get there? The Report of the High-level Panel casts some light on these questions.[2] In order to appreciate its conclusions and omissions, it helps to see them in light of the interpretation of the Charter that prevailed in the immediate aftermath of the Charter's adoption.

At the birth of the United Nations, a majority of legal scholars and probably of governments subscribed to the view that taking into account the language and structure of the Charter, in particular Articles 2(4) and 51 in conjunction with Chapter VII as a whole, and taking into account also the document's negotiating history, it should be read as dividing the universe of cross-border military coercion and intervention into three categories. Category 1 is self-defence against an armed attack. Category 2 is force (or the threat thereof) authorized by the Security Council (SC) under Chapter VII to prevent a threat to the peace, a breach of the peace or an act of aggression. The domain of the illegal is Category 3—call it the default category, which is occupied by every act of state-initiated or tolerated cross-border violence that does not fall into the first two categories.[3] However, it was not long before states with the capacity to project force across frontiers began proposing additional categories, based in part on curious readings of the Charter, that happened to legitimate their uses of force, and they invariably found some scholars who sympathized with their claims. What follows is a sketch of the areas of ambiguity and contention.

What constitutes an "armed attack" for purposes of activating the right of individual and collective self-defence?

a. *Do activities short of launching troops, planes, or missiles across a frontier, for instance giving material assistance to an insurgency in another state or a terrorist group, ever trigger the right of self-defence?*

During the Cold War, primarily with respect to the guerrilla wars against pro-Western regimes in Latin America and Southeast Asia, the US argued that where State A provided weapons or training to opponents of the recognized government of State B, the latter and allied states could treat that assistance as an armed attack. The World Court rejected this claim in the Nicaragua case insofar as it purported to justify US acts of war within Nicaragua.

b. *At what point, if any, do activities that could reasonably be construed as preparations to launch an armed attack, justify pre-emption?*

Perhaps because on a number of occasions during the Cold War, mechanical and electronic devices erroneously signalled the launch of nuclear missiles, some have argued that pre-emption should never be allowed, that self-defence requires a prior and actual border crossing. But efforts to base a definition of aggression on first recourse to force under all circumstances failed. The more generally prevailing view seemed to be that if the behaviour of State A is such as to lead a reasonable commander in State B to believe that an armed and substantial attack is imminent and cannot be averted by means other than force, State B may pre-empt.

Most scholars regarded *imminence* as the key criterion. Without it, measures reasonably intended for defensive purposes could be construed by another, unfriendly state as preparations for an attack justifying a first strike. That is why the Bush administration's declaration of an intent to strike unfriendly states whenever they engage in behaviour evidencing preparations designed to facilitate an attack against the United States at some future time could not under this view be reconciled with the Charter.[4] The Bush doctrine actually restates the rationale for *preventive*, not pre-emptive, wars, the kinds of wars urged, for instance, by German strategists in the late nineteenth and early twentieth centuries, fearing the long-term military superiority of the continental powers, Russia, and the United States.

c. *Can forms of coercion other than military ones constitute an armed attack?*

Developing states have sometimes argued that economic ones threatening their political independence should be so regarded. The US seemed to imply the same during the Arab oil boycott following the 1973 Middle East War. In the West, there was little if any scholarly support for this view and efforts to include economic coercion in the definition of aggression failed.

Does the Security Council have authority under the Charter to authorize coercive measures including use of force in cases (a) where the threat to international peace and security is not imminent or (b) the "threat" consists of massive violations of human rights within a country but with little immediate spillover effect to other states?

With respect to (a), two views once competed for dominance. Some commentators argued that the Council was an organ with jurisdictional authority strictly limited by the language of the Charter and that the Charter's grant of authority under Chapter VII to deal coercively with "threats" had to be read in the light of Chapter VI authorizing the Council to employ non-coercive measures like mediation in cases where a situation could develop into a threat. In other words, the Charter itself distinguishes in so many words between immediate and potential or longer-term threats and gives the Council authority to employ force only in the latter case. So while it has authority to employ force (or to authorize force by states acting as its proxy) at a somewhat earlier point than an individual state can under Article 51, that authority does not extend to cases where the threat is in so early a stage of incubation that its actualization is uncertain and there is opportunity to test the efficacy of means other than force.

I have seen little support in recent years for this view in Western academic circles, although it may well reflect the preferences of the Chinese and certain other governments in the global South. While the Council may not have absolute discretion to define its authority, it has and in contemporary circumstances must have a very broad discretion to decide at what stage in the gestation of a threat it should intervene with coercive means of one form or another.

With respect to (b), the practice of the Council since the end of the Cold War seems to have resolved the once sharp dispute over its authority to intervene in catastrophes that occur mainly within one country. When in the 1970s it authorized coercive measures against the minority racist regime in what was then Rhodesia (contemporary Zimbabwe), the Council was sharply criticized by some legal commentators and initially the United Kingdom took the position that the matter was an internal concern.[5] Sanctions against South Africa in the 1980s also encountered some opposition on legal grounds. Since the Cold War, however, the Council has authorized intervention to restore democracy (Haiti), to protect the delivery of humanitarian relief (Bosnia and Somalia, for instance), and to end civil conflicts marked by massive violations of human rights (Sierra Leone, for instance). Practice has confirmed the breadth of the Council's power to act for the sake of human as well as national security.

Can regional and sub-regional organizations authorize uses of force that would otherwise be illegal?

Articles 52–54 (Chapter VIII) of the Charter recognize a possible role for such organizations particularly in helping to mediate festering hostility that, if left unattended, could lead to armed conflict. It also rec-

ognizes them as possible instruments of the Security Council in dealing with Chapter VII situations. But Article 54 states that any "enforcement action" by such organizations requires the approval of the Security Council.

During the Cold War, the US argued (in relation to the Cuban Quar-
antine of 1962, the intervention into the Dominican Republic in 1965,
and the invasion of Grenada in 1982) that the approval could be after
the fact and implicit, a position most scholars and governments
rejected.[6] In recent years, the US has altered its position insofar as the
Organization of American States (OAS) is concerned, insisting (most
clearly in the case of Haiti) that enforcement measures require SC
authorization. But the first ECOWAS intervention in Liberia, although
not authorized, was not criticized, much less condemned. A distinguished panel of experts established by the Swedish government found
NATO's intervention in the Kosovo conflict to be not consistent with
the Charter and thus technically illegal but nevertheless "legitimate."[7]
Whether NATO, originally a self-defence rather than regional organization, can be said to have evolved into the latter is open to dispute.

**Does armed intervention at the request of a recognized government
to assist it in repressing armed domestic opponents constitute
a permitted use of force?**

Some scholars and governments have argued that the prerogatives of
sovereignty certainly include authorizing foreign intervention and that
the recognized government is the agent of state sovereignty. Others
have said that in cases of large-scale civil war, an intervention, even if
invited by the recognized government, violates the country's political
independence and the universal right of self-determination and should
be deemed illegal.

**Are interventions, not authorized by the SC but undertaken to
prevent or terminate crimes against humanity, ever legal
under the Charter?**

In the early decades after the Charter's adoption, scholars and governments especially were reluctant to concede that the claims of humanity might trump the principle of non-intervention, although at least in
particular cases some seemed disposed to treat the circumstances as
highly mitigating. The Kosovo Commission mentioned above based
its finding of "legitimacy" largely on what it perceived as the imperative necessity of using force in order to abort massive ethnic cleansing
already initiated, in its view, by the Belgrade Government against the

Albanian ethnic population of Kosovo. Few would dispute that mass ethnic cleansing is a "crime against humanity," with genocidal potential. With respect to the question of law, it is significant that even in the presence of such a crime, coupled with action by an arguably "regional organization" (but not, to be sure against a *member* of the organization) and SC resolutions condemning the government of ex-Yugoslavia for its treatment of the Albanian population and calling upon it to cease and desist, a committee of experts with a strong collective commitment to the protection of human rights finds that action, although legitimate, to be illegal under the Charter. Nevertheless, some leading primarily US-based international law scholars, including ardent defenders of the UN and the Charter-based legal order, have argued that humanitarian intervention is legal where the following criteria are satisfied:

- a massive crime against humanity is imminent or has begun to be executed;
- either there is no time for recourse to the SC, if the crime is to be averted or aborted before its completion, or action by the SC is blocked by a Permanent Member's exercise of its veto;
- the action is reported to the SC;
- the intervention is carried out in good faith and so as to minimize its consequences for the political independence of the target state; and
- the intervention complies with the Humanitarian Law of War and is reasonably calculated to cause less harm to "innocent persons" than would occur if the crime against humanity were allowed to proceed.[8]

Scholars insisting on the legality of interventions satisfying the above criteria emphasized the Charter's recognition of human rights along with national sovereignty as paired constitutional principles. Even scholars from countries with a history of intense opposition to intervention of any kind now show some disposition to concede that in extraordinary circumstances, for example the onset of genocide, international action may be justified even if the SC does not authorize it. A number of Chinese scholars from influential think tanks have so conceded in a recent discussion, but they insisted that circumstances must be so exceptional that they cannot be codified, a position echoing that of the leading English authority on the use of force, Ian Brownlie, who analogized humanitarian interventions to "mercy killings" in domestic law which are illegal but may be overlooked in extraordinary circumstances.[9] Efforts by the Axworthy Commission, supported by the Canadian Government, to promote agreement that the prerogatives of sovereignty are dependent in some measure on states meeting minimum obligations to their citizens initially met a cool reception from the generality of governments, implying that they preferred the Chinese approach.[10]

The humanitarian arguments invoked by the US and the UK in the case of Iraq, arguments increasingly emphasized when evidence of WMD programs failed to appear, are unusual in that they refer to conditions that were chronic rather than acute. In fact, at the time of the invasion, violations of core human security rights appear to have been considerably less acute than during earlier periods when popular resistance to Saddam was more pronounced. The moral basis for distinguishing chronic violations of rights from acute ones, as most advocates of humanitarian intervention do, is problematical.

Are interventions strictly to rescue nationals arbitrarily threatened with death or grave injury, whether by the government of another country or by private groups whom that government cannot or will not control, legal under the Charter?

Some scholars have long insisted that intervention as a last resort for the protection of threatened nationals falls under the right to self-defence. They note that a state consists of a determinate territory and a population. Attacks on either, they argue, are "armed attacks" within the meaning of Article 51 of the Charter. It is also argued that such brief interventions, proportional to the imperative necessity of extracting the threatened persons, should not be regarded as violations of either the territorial integrity or the political independence of the target state and hence not violations of Article 2, paragraph 4 of the Charter. That argument rests implicitly on a view much like that of the Axworthy Commission, namely that by failing to meet their international legal obligations to protect the nationals of other states, states to that extent relinquish temporarily the full prerogatives of sovereignty.

Are reprisals legal under the Charter?

In pre-Charter international legal practice, reprisals were punitive acts responding to some illegal act committed by another state. They were deemed legitimate if they were proportional to the delinquency that occasioned them. One of their recognized purposes was to deter a repetition of the delinquency. In relation to a reprisal carried out by the

United Kingdom during the 1950s in what is today the Republic of Yemen, the Security Council declared reprisals to be illegal under the Charter in that they did not constitute acts of self-defence.[11] Self-defence presumed an ongoing attack. A one-off border incursion by forces of State A into State B could be resisted. But if State A's forces withdrew before State B could mount a response and appeared unlikely to make another incursion in the immediate future, then the opportunity for the exercise of self-defence rights had passed. State B would thus have to pursue other remedies for any damage done to it from the incursion including, of course, an appeal to the Security Council on the grounds that the situation constitutes an ongoing "threat to the peace."

Distinguishing reprisal and legitimate self-defence can be difficult in the context of ongoing hostile relations between states marked by numerous "incidents." For instance, the bombing of Tripoli by the United States in the wake of the bombing of a nightclub in Berlin frequented by US military personnel and attributed to Libyan intelligence operatives was arguably a reprisal; but the US could have argued that the bombing was only one in a line of Libyan-organized attacks on US installations and personnel and that these various incidents amounted cumulatively to an ongoing attack. Similarly, some Israeli incursions into neighbouring Arab states could have been characterized as incidents in a single ongoing low-intensity armed conflict. However, Israel has an explicit doctrine of reprisal; it has not tried to characterize every incursion as an incident of an ongoing war. And many of its reprisals have been ignored by the SC or action has been blocked by the US.

It appears that the SC has become inured to reprisals, at least in the Arab-Israeli context, and therefore takes note of them only where they risk igniting a general conflict or possibly where they are grossly disproportionate to the damage inflicted by the act held to justify reprisal or violate rights protected by the humanitarian law of war. It did not condemn the US missile attack on Iraq following the alleged attempt by Saddam Hussein to assassinate former President George H.W. Bush during a visit to Kuwait. Arguably that was a reprisal, although it might have been defended as mere enforcement of the terms of the ceasefire that ended the first Gulf War.

To help probe the distinction between acts justifying reprisal and acts of war, I offer the following hypothetical case. Suppose the attack on the World Trade Center and the Pentagon on 11 September 2001 had been the first violent act against US persons or property by persons under the direction of Osama Bin Laden and his associates and had been accompanied by a statement from Bin Laden describing it as a single retaliation for crimes committed against the Arab people and declaring that the slate was clean, there had been an eye-for-an-eye, and now coexistence was possible. If, without benefit of an SC resolution recognizing the availability of the claim of self-defence under the circumstances, the US had launched its campaign to overturn the Taliban regime and to destroy Bin Laden's infrastructure in Afghanistan and to kill or capture Bin Laden and his lieutenants, would that have been a reprisal or lawful action in self-defence under the Charter?

It is implausible that, under those circumstances, the US or any other nation that had experienced such a blow would have felt constrained either by the Charter or even by the pre-Charter doctrine to treat that blow as something other than an act of war. As an act of war, an aggression against the US, it would presumably allow the United States to take all necessary measures consistent with the Humanitarian Law of War to capture or kill the perpetrators and to dismantle their organization and to wage war against any state that interfered in this effort. In other words, some acts of violence may be of such scope and intensity that states generally will probably regard them as acts of war even if it is unclear that they will be repeated.

What limits does the Charter impose on the right of self-defence once it is triggered by an act of aggression?
The hypothetical case in the previous question raises two further questions. One is whether, in a case where following a wanton act of aggression the aggressor withdraws from any territory it may have occupied and places its forces in a defensive posture and calls for negotiation or mediation of whatever dispute occasioned the aggression, the victim state can initiate a defensive war without SC authorization even though it can seek such authorization without further endangering itself. The second is whether a state exercising its right of self-defence by preparing to invade an aggressor or destroy its military capability through an assault by missiles and aircraft must desist in cases where the SC, acting pursuant to Chapter VII, authorizes less intense measures such as economic sanctions or a blockade to force the surrender of the persons authorizing and conducting the aggression or takes other action which the victim state deems insufficient. Neither the practice of states and of the Security Council under the Charter nor the opinions of international legal experts has provided entirely clear answers to either question.

THE VIEWS OF THE HIGH-LEVEL PANEL

The Panel attempts to resolve some but by no means all of the contentious issues sketched above.

On the present legal status of the Charter's use-of-force constraints

Overall, the Panel's views appear to fall somewhere between those who argue that the Charter's use-of-force regime remains legally binding much as originally construed and those who believe it has collapsed. But in one respect it goes further than some contemporary sceptics in discounting the legal force of the Charter. Here is the relevant Panel language:

> For the first 44 years of the United Nations, member states often violated these rules and used military force literally hundreds of times...and Article 51 only rarely providing credible cover. Since the end of the Cold War, however, the yearning for an international system governed by the rule of law has grown.[12]

These words imply that the Charter's use-of-force rules collapsed as a legal regime within a few years of their adoption in 1945, the Cold War being conventionally dated from 1949. But in contrast to today's rule skeptics, it sees not an intensification of indifference to but rather a strengthened desire ("yearning") for legal restraint. Complementing that yearning is something approaching a negative consensus (with the United States as the main possible holdout) in opposition to the merely de facto restraints of a balance of power system or to a security system legislated and policed "by any single—even benignly motivated—superpower."[13] Moreover, the Report states that "expectations about legal compliance" with the Charter constraints (essentially as initially construed) "are very much higher [today]."[14]

In his 21 March 2005 Report to the General Assembly, the Secretary General takes a similar nuanced position, stating that the Charter "as it stands offers a good basis for the understanding [among states about the use of force] that we need."[15] That is a good deal less than a ringing affirmation that the Charter rules on the use of force are declarative of international law.

What constitutes an "armed attack" under Article 51?

While recognizing that the potential for catastrophic attack by terrorists has sharply intensified threats to national and human security, the

Panel nevertheless adheres to the original view that resort to force without Security Council authorization is unacceptable where a threat is not imminent.[16] For if it is not imminent, then there is time to have recourse to the Council. To be sure, the Panel concedes, "the Council's decisions have been less than consistent, less than persuasive and less than fully responsive to very real State and human security needs." The answer to the resulting dilemma for states that feel deeply threatened, the Panel argues, is not unilateral action but reform of the Council.

Do regional and sub-regional organizations have an independent authority to legitimate the use of force in the absence of Security Council action?

The Panel fails to resolve the present uncertainty or to clarify divergent practice. It merely says that the one exception other than self-defence to the Charter's prohibition of the use of force in Article 2(4) is "military measures authorized by the Security Council under Chapter VII (*and by extension for* [sic] *regional organizations under Chapter VIII)* [emphasis added]."[17] The recently published Report of the Secretary General to the General Assembly, which to a considerable degree tracks the Panel Report, deals at much greater length with the relationship between regional organizations and the UN but also fails to state unambiguously that such organizations do or do not have independent authorizing power.

Does the Security Council have a broad authority to authorize the preventive use of force in matters concerning relations between states?

The Panel seems fully in accord with those who find such authority in the Charter. Not only does it recognize Charter authority for preventive action, it suggests that that authority may be read more broadly today than in the past. (Council may well have to take more decisive action "earlier than...in the past"[18]). The Panel illustrates preventive action with the hypothesized case of a state that has expressed hostility to another state suddenly acquiring nuclear weapon-making capability. Even without evidence of any intention to use or to seek concessions by threatening to use that capability, the Council could, in the Panel members' view, find a threat to the peace and therefore act or authorize action pursuant to Chapter VII.[19]

Does the Security Council have broad authority to authorize force, preventive or otherwise, where crimes against humanity are threatened or are occurring within a state?

The Panel's answer is unambiguously affirmative. The almost universally ratified Genocide Convention evidenced decades ago the broadly shared conviction that the principle of non-intervention declared in Article 2(7) of the Charter cannot be used to protect perpetrators or crimes against humanity. In other words, they can and should be considered threats to international security. Revealing the Panel's temper in this respect, and therefore of the sea change that has occurred in the perceptions and values of official elites, is the Panel's equation of national and "human" security, a juxtaposition of concepts—indeed of words—rarely heard in official discourse before the end of the Cold War. The Panel reinforces its position by citing "growing recognition that the issue is not the 'right to intervene' of any state, but the 'responsibility to protect' of *every* state when it comes to people suffering from avoidable catastrophe—mass murder and rape, ethnic cleansing by forcible expulsion and terror, and deliberate starvation and exposure to disease."[20] States that either choose not to meet that responsibility or simply lack the capacity to protect temporarily lose to that extent the normal insulation of sovereignty. The Panel recognizes and endorses an "emerging norm of a collective international responsibility to protect."[21]

If the Council fails to act or crimes against humanity are imminent or already occurring, is unilateral action (i.e., "Humanitarian intervention") legal or legitimate?

On this question, the Panel, obviously anxious to encourage collective action and critical of past inaction, is silent.

The relationship of legality and legitimacy

Like the Swedish government-funded Kosovo Commission, the Panel distinguishes between the legal and the legitimate use of force; but unlike the Commission, which was considering the propriety of force unauthorized by the Council, it does so only with respect to Security Council action, and preventive action at that. Thus it again avoids the question of humanitarian intervention.

When it first considers the legitimacy issue, the Panel appears to introduce a third criterion for evaluating Council action, namely "prudence": "Questions of legality apart, there will be issues of prudence, or legitimacy."[22] Could the report be saying that prudence is the essence of legitimacy? I think not, in part because when it again turns to the issue, this time for a more detailed discussion, the Panel appears to treat prudence simply as *one* of the tests of the legitimacy of a Council decision.[23]

I reach this conclusion by tracking the sequence of the Panel's arguments in this subsection on "The Question of Legitimacy." It begins with the assertion that the "effectiveness of the global collective security system...depends ultimately not only on the legality of decisions but also on the common perception of their legitimacy—their being made on solid evidentiary grounds [sic], and for the right reasons, morally as well as legally" [note the absence here of any reference to "prudence."][24] Then the Panel says: "in deciding whether or not to authorize the use of force, the Council should adopt and systematically address a set of agreed guidelines, going directly not to whether force *can* legally be used but whether, as a matter of good conscience and good sense, it *should* be."[25] Finally, in paragraph 206 it sets out five guidelines that closely track the criteria for a just war widely recognized by moralists from Aquinas to contemporary thinkers. They include "Balance of Consequences" (Is there a reasonable chance of the military action being successful in meeting the threat in question, with the consequences of action not likely to be worse than the consequences of inaction?"). The last of the five proposed criteria seems to be essentially identical to the classical just war criterion of "prudence" or "reasonable judgment." In short, prudence is an element of legitimacy, not a separate criterion.

FINAL COMMENTS

1. *A less than complete treatment of use-of-force issues*: Obviously the Panel dealt only with what, in the light of the Kosovo intervention and the invasion of Iraq, reasonably appeared to it as the most consequential of the various use-of-force issues enumerated in the first part of this paper. The issues it passed over are not Cold War relics. They will recur. However, if the Security Council becomes the linchpin of the collective security system, acting consistently and effectively to address all cases that substantially engage international and human security, then it will doubtless resolve case-by-case the issues ignored by the Panel as they arise.

2. *Humanitarian Emergencies vs. Cases of Chronic Violation*: Most proposed guidelines for legitimate humanitarian intervention have included what I have elsewhere called the "spike test," i.e., a dramatic

increase in the breadth and possibly the severity of human rights violations as distinguished from the quotidian torture, mutilation, arbitrary imprisonment and murder that characterize many tyrannical regimes like that of the deposed Saddam Hussein. The distinction does not have immediate moral appeal. For it could insulate regimes like Saddam's that are so effective in terrorizing the population that, except where external conflict weakens the regime's grip, it can endure for years without meeting the spike test. Yet over time it may well ruin far more lives than a regime that at one moment in time satisfies that test, as the Milosevic regime seemed to at the time of NATO's Kosovo intervention (admittedly some argue that mass ethnic cleansing was a response to the bombing). Be that as it may, the Panel's first criterion of legitimacy appears to adopt the spike test ("In the case of internal threats, does [the threatened harm] include genocide and other large-scale killing, ethnic cleansing or serious violations of international humanitarian law, actual or imminently apprehended"). To be sure, that would have justified Security Council authorization of intervention in Iraq for the genocidal assault on the Kurds during the Iran-Iraq war and on the Shia in the aftermath of Desert Storm.

3. *Military measures as the "last resort" and "proportional means" as "military action of the minimum necessary to meet the threat in question"*: There are interpretations of these two criteria that are politically correct in the traditional UN context and there are interpretations that persons with at least a modest concern for human security should prefer. The "last-resort" test asks whether "every non-military option for meeting the threat in question [has] been explored, with reasonable grounds for believing that other measures will not succeed." From the perspective of human security, the better test, I suggest, is *whether early resort to military means that are available is the most likely way of aborting the threat at least cost to the intended beneficiaries of the intervention.*

The "proportional means" test, as traditionally construed, inhibits the international community from the root-and-branch reordering of the target government and possibly the society that the very severity of the humanitarian emergency suggests may well be necessary in order to prevent its recurrence. In the traditional construction, the intervention was designed to halt genocidal or mass killing, have minimal impact on social and political structures, and end as soon as the killing had stopped and there was no prospect of its imminent renewal. Concern for long-term occupation and deep political and social restructuring may well be appropriate in the case of unilateral or coalition interventions, where humanitarian concern may cloak more parochial motives. Where the Security Council authorizes intervention that concern seems inapplicable.

NOTES

1 See, e.g., Michael Glennon, "The New Interventionism," *Foreign Affairs* May/June 1999, 2–7.
2 *A More Secure World: Our Shared Responsibility*, Report of the Secretary General's High-level Panel on Threats, Challenges and Change, UN Doc. A/59/565. Online at http://www.un.org/secureworld/report2.pdf.
3 See, e.g., Tom Farer, "Human Rights in Law's Empire: The Jurisprudence War," *American Journal of International Law* 85, 1 (January 1991): 117–27; and "A Paradigm of Legitimate Intervention," in Lori Fisler Damrosch, ed., *Enforcing Restraint: Collective Intervention in Internal Conflicts* (New York: Council on Foreign Relations, 1993), 316–45.
4 Tom Farer, "Agora: Future Implications of the Iraq Conflict," *American Journal of International Law* 97, 3 (July 2003): 621–28.
5 Dean Acheson so argued and was criticized by McDougal and Reisman in "Rhodesia and the United Nations: The Lawfulness of International Concern," *American Journal of International Law* 62, 1 (January 1968): 1–19.
6 Tom Farer, "The Role of Regional Collective Security Arrangements," in *Collective Security in a Changing World*, T. Weiss, ed., (Boulder: Lynne Rienner, 1993), 153–88.
7 The Commission was also endorsed by UN Secretary General Kofi Annan. Full text of the report can be found at http://www.reliefweb.int/library/documents/thekosovoreport.htm.
8 These views are reflected in J.L. Holzgrefe and R.O. Keohane (eds.), *Humanitarian Intervention: Ethical, Legal and Political Dilemmas* (Cambridge: Cambridge University Press, 2002).
9 Ian Brownlie, *International Law and the Use of Force by States* (Oxford: Clarendon Press, 1963).
10 International Commission on Intervention and State Sovereignty, *The Responsibility to Protect* (Ottawa: International Development Research Centre, 2001).
11 Tom Farer, "Law and War," in C.E. Black and R.A. Falk (eds.), *The Future of the International Legal Order: Conflict Management*, vol. 3 (Princeton: Princeton University Press, 1969), 15–78.
12 HLP, paragraph 186.
13 HLP, paragraph 186.
14 The view of the law implicit in the third section of the Report is plainly informed by contemporary jurisprudence which recognizes that law is a matter of degree—the degree of consensus about its existence and application in given issue areas.
15 HLP, paragraph 123.
16 HLP, paragraphs 193–198.

17 HLP, paragraph 185.
18 HLP, paragraph 194.
19 HLP, paragraph 188.
20 HLP, paragraph 201.
21 HLP, paragraphs 202–203.
22 HLP, paragraph 195.
23 HLP, paragraphs 204–209.
24 HLP, paragraph 204.
25 HLP, paragraph 205.

10 SMALL ARMS, BIG KILLERS

INTRODUCTION

The central challenge today facing Afghanistan, Iraq, Sudan (Darfur), the Democratic Republic of Congo, Haiti, Colombia, and several other states is arguably insecurity stemming primarily (but not exclusively) from the proliferation and misuse of small arms and light weapons.[1] The ability to establish public order, to deliver humanitarian relief, to maintain basic government services (schools, clinics, food distribution points, etc.), to establish political stability, and to launch more ambitious development and reconstruction efforts is over and over held hostage to organized violence on a small and large scale, in these and many other states.

One could unpack each of the major conflict situations around the world—some in a violent, others in a quiescent, phase—and attribute the root causes to a variety of complex factors. The quest for root causes and underlying factors is not nearly as important though—from the point of view of designing effective and cost-efficient policy interventions—as focusing on the tools of violence, the small arms and light weapons that are in the wrong hands, and that are used on a daily basis to threaten, injure and kill.

There are more than 640 million small arms and light weapons in circulation worldwide, a large percentage of which are legally held or which are not likely to be used to cause harm. But the weapons that are misused are probably responsible for at least 300,000 (and likely more), deaths each year, and a significantly higher number of injuries, with enormous short- and long-term economic, social, and human costs. As the Inter-American Development Bank estimated, the direct and indirect costs of violence in Latin America amounted to US$140-170 billion per year.

Perhaps more than half of these deaths do *not* occur in conflict zones—but from a human security perspective, this is irrelevant, and the distinction between war and everyday forms of insecurity is increasingly blurring in many places around the world.

Addressing the proliferation and misuse of small arms and light weapons means breaking out of some old modes of thinking, and recognizing some distinct features of the problem. I will summarize these in four points, which I will develop and illustrate below. I should say that most examples and cases are drawn from the five years of extensive research and analysis of the *Small Arms Survey*, an independent non-governmental research institute based at the Graduate Institute of International Studies, in Geneva, Switzerland.[2] My fourth—and longest—point will attempt to answer directly the question of what role the United Nations can and should play in the panoply of efforts to address the small arms and light weapons challenge.

My central points are that:

1. Small arms and light weapons do not represent *one* problem, but rather a cluster of different issues grouped under one umbrella. In this respect, the problem of small arms is a challenge to global public policy of the same order as global warming, rather than a discrete problem such as thinning of the ozone layer.

2. Small arms should not be understood as an "arms control and disarmament" issue, subject to comprehensive international restraint and treaty-based measures. The "arms control" approach represents one aspect among many in the policy tool-kit.

3. Small arms are *social artefacts*, and as such are usually—unlike other types of weapons—embedded in complex social systems, and a nuanced understanding of the social and economic context of weapons possession and use is essential to effective policy-making.

4. Tackling the problem of small arms requires "multi-level" governance, from the global to the local level. The most important measures that can be developed are often national in nature, but these must be embedded in robust regional and global regimes to regulate the cross-border or external consequences of national policies.

SMALL ARMS: NOT ONE ISSUE, BUT MANY INTER-RELATED ISSUES

Colombia, a country long in the thrall of a bitter ideological conflict, has among the world's highest rates of firearm deaths. Yet only 20 percent of the more than 20,000 annual deaths from firearms occur as a result of the ongoing conflict; the vast majority are associated with high levels of criminal violence. The picture is even more dramatic in Brazil, where firearms violence claims about 30,000 victims a year, and the murder rate of 29 per 100,000 is also among the world's highest. In both these cases, armed violence is overwhelmingly crime-related, inextricably linked to drug gangs, urban slums, and youth violence.[3]

In Liberia, by contrast, the problem of small arms is a result of the long civil war, which in the 1990s dissolved into warlord politics. Current policies on small arms are linked to the problem of post-conflict disarmament and demobilization, where somewhere between 38,000 and 100,000 ex-combatants have been engaged in a so-far incomplete process of disarmament, demobilization, and reintegration (DDR). The disarmament process collected 27,000 weapons, although operational difficulties resulted in several riots and a great deal of frustration. This, plus a shortage of funds, has meant that Liberian armed groups remain organized and violence still threatens the peace process.[4] In Iraq, the ongoing conflict has probably—according to the only robust epidemiological study conducted in the country—claimed more than 30,000 lives due to armed violence, and perhaps up to 100,000 dead, from what the health profession euphemistically calls "excess mortality."[5] It hardly needs saying that rampant insecurity and instability is connected to the widespread availability and misuse of weapons in Iraqi society.

When we turn to East-Central Europe—to Ukraine, Belarus, or Russia itself, the problem is the massive excessive stockpiles of weapons that are a hangover from Soviet days. Ukraine, for example, has recently agreed under NATO's Euro-Atlantic Partnership Council (EAPC) auspices to destroy more than 1.5 million surplus weapons, in the largest single weapons destruction program to be conducted. But it will take several years to achieve even this, and it is widely acknowledged that the actual volume of excess stocks is at least seven million (and perhaps more than twelve million) weapons.[6] If even a small fraction of these arms were to be sold on the international market, they could fuel a number of small wars and wreak havoc in countless communities.

These three examples illustrate that the problem of small arms is *not* one problem. In some places, it is linked to organized criminal violence, in others to ongoing conflicts, in still others the problem is one of stockpile security, export controls, and destruction of surplus weapons stocks.

It is not surprising, therefore, that there does not exist a single policy solution to the problem at the international level. Those who expected that the small arms issue represented an easy follow-on to international action to eliminate the threat of anti-personnel land mines were disappointed, but it would be wrong to conclude that the absence of an international agreement (other than the comprehensive, but only weakly politically binding, UN Programme of Action) means that the problem is not being addressed in a coherent and comprehensive way. The complexity of the problem means, however, that we have to think about the challenges that small arms pose for our entire conception of "global governance" or "global public policy."[7]

LIMITS OF THE ARMS CONTROL AND SECURITY APPROACH

The small arms issue includes not just an international security (and arms control) dimension, but is also a concern for the criminal justice, public health, development, human rights, and humanitarian relief communities. But stating this does not help us to see what the appropriate tools and approaches might be for tackling the problem. In fact, to date the diplomacy of small arms has been mainly associated with a security-oriented process, developed around the New York diplomatic community.

Seen from Geneva, this is dysfunctional in several ways. First, the important roles that could be played by the development, humanitarian and public health communities—to name the most relevant—are downgraded or occluded. Second, the diplomatic mechanisms (such as the role for NGO representation, or the way in which documents are negotiated), draw upon other arms control and disarmament processes, and tend therefore to limit the scope for other perspectives and approaches. More importantly, the "reflex" of the security community is to think about negotiated, legally binding, verifiable and universalizable instruments, whose short- or medium-term goal would be the suffocation or reduction of the global supply of these weapons.

Yet there are very few aspects of the small arms problématique that are susceptible to this approach, for two reasons. First, the negative externalities that are caused by small arms proliferation and misuse are heavily weighted to the national and regional level—the spillover effects beyond one region to another are less important, except in areas such as export controls, arms brokering, marking and tracing of weapons, and (to a limited extent) stockpile security and destruction of surplus stocks. These are important (and I will discuss at least one of them below), but they are not the alpha and omega of the problem.

Second, and from a practical point of view, it is neither feasible nor desirable to regulate the more than 600 million small arms and light weapons in circulation. Most (but not all) of the weapons of major concern are those that have "slipped" from the legal to the illicit circuit, and are now found in the hands of irregular armies, communal factions, crime and drug syndicates, gangs, individual criminals, and so forth. Again, legally or politically binding interstate instruments by themselves will not address most aspects of this problem. Effective implementation must take place at the regional, national and local levels, and real improvements in capacity (police forces, criminal justice systems, customs controls) must occur at these levels.

WHAT MAKES SMALL ARMS SO DIFFICULT TO ADDRESS?

Arms are instruments of power, designed to wound or kill. Yet they are also cultural and social artefacts that have legitimate and illegitimate uses implicating honour, prestige, masculinity, protection, power and, of course, the ability to cause harm. The result is that different social and cultural attitudes towards weapons possession result in very different regulatory and control mechanisms. A simple comparison between Canadian, Australian, British, and American (to pick states only in the English-speaking world) views on gun control will confirm this. This has two important consequences that must be kept in mind.

First, there is no simple equation between weapons availability and misuse. Any relationship that does exist is mediated through economic and social factors that are highly contextual. Switzerland, for example, has relatively widespread ownership of weapons, and the famous militia weapon in the basement of most able-bodied men's homes. Yet the result is not rampant insecurity and misuse (although on some variables, such as suicide, weapons use is a bit more prevalent than in neighbouring states). Other states such as Canada, Norway, and Finland also have high levels of civilian possession. Britain, by contrast, is extremely restrictive, yet appears to have experienced a surge in armed violence in major cities, in part driven by weapons smuggling in from continental Europe.

Second, and related, there is an important difference between a "gun culture" and a "culture of violence." Traditional so-called gun cultures often, in fact, place a premium on the symbolic or non-violent uses of weapons, and on their importance for traditional activities such as hunting or sport. The practices associated with traditional gun cultures (such as passing weapons from fathers to sons, or ceremonial shooting) often erode with rural-urban migration and social modernization.[8] Cultures of violence, by contrast, can be bred in urban slums, linked to the activities of drug gangs and a general breakdown of the criminal justice system, and there is nothing particularly "traditional" about this. When one recognizes that fewer than 20 percent of the murders committed in Brazil with firearms are *even brought into the court system*, let alone successfully prosecuted, it is clear that a climate of judicial impunity exists that fuels and reinforces the culture of violence and insecurity.[9] This may be more important than any so-called cultural factors.

WHAT IS TO BE DONE (BY THE UN AND OTHERS)?

There is a limited set of issues on which international agreement— broad, but not necessarily universal—would be desirable, in order for national and local policies to be "embedded" within a robust international framework. Three such measures stand out:

- harmonized regulation of the activities of arms brokers;
- a strong international instrument on marking and tracing of illicit weapons; and
- a reinforced international export control regime.

In each case, one or two "champion" states have been identified: the Netherlands and Norway are leading consultations on international arms brokering; Switzerland is chairing the working group to negotiate an international instrument on marking and tracing, and the UK has been very active in promoting enhanced export controls, via the EU, and more broadly. In each case, they have worked hand in hand with non-governmental partners to promote their initiatives—a lesson that should be kept in mind for all such initiatives.

But three things need to be recognized about these (and other) instruments. First, they are measures designed to shift the "costs and benefits" of illicit transfers and use of small arms—they do not destroy weapons or remove them from society, nor do they reduce production or stockpiles. Thus, although they are a crucial part of the puzzle, they depend on other, more concrete, measures in order to be truly effective. Second, and more importantly, we should not think that we have solved the problem of small arms just because such instruments have been created.

Third, because they are designed to make it more difficult or costly, for example, to traffic in weapons, or to retransfer them from one conflict or another, or to increase criminal penalties for such transactions, they do *not* need to be universal to be effective. Even measures with limited scope, if the relevant producers and suppliers can be brought in—or neutralized through naming and shaming—will have some effect. And in the streets of Freetown or Rio or Manila, this might be the most important thing, making the quest for verifiable, legally binding, universal treaties a bit beside the point.

In addition to this (limited) role for negotiating legally or politically binding agreements in areas where broad international action is required, there are two other areas in which UN involvement in addressing the problem of small arms proliferation and misuse is crucial:

- norm-setting and the dissemination of "best practices" for regional and national legislation and regulation;[10]
- the incorporation of a small arms component into *all* humanitarian relief and post-conflict reconstruction and development programs.

The first of these recognizes that the most important practical measures are *national* policies and regulations, and that the regulatory framework governing small arms proliferation and misuse is very weak in many parts of the world. Much basic assistance needs to be provided to states so that they can identify which arms, in whose hands, pose the greatest threat to the safety and security of their citizens. Serious research is also needed in order to design evidence-based policies, rather than just ad hoc diagnoses that are likely to "miss the target."

The second builds on the now-extensive experience of the UN, mainly through the Bureau for Crisis Prevention and Reconstruction of the UN Development Programme, with post-conflict disarmament programs. More than a dozen such programs have been launched under UN auspices (in places such as Niger, Solomon Islands, Albania, Kosovo, Republic of Congo, and elsewhere) and more, such as in Cambodia, under other organizational umbrellas. The detailed lessons of these projects are too numerous to list here, but one fundamental point that has been recognized is that a failure to address directly the small arms issue can seriously undermine broader peacebuilding and post-conflict development policies. The equation is simple: without a basic level of security and safety, development and reconstruction are difficult if not impossible, and a small arms program is an essential component of any sensible security-building policy.

It is important that we keep in mind that the issue of small arms is a truly "multi-dimensional, multi-level" challenge. The role of a "top-down" organization such as the UN is a limited one, and human security is built mainly through the interaction between states and their citizens. The true test of any of the measures I have listed above is therefore ultimately whether or not people are safer and more secure in their homes, neighbourhoods and communities. We are a long way to realizing this, but if we keep this goal in mind, we will be able to design practical and effective policy initiatives, at whatever level of governance is appropriate, to address this urgent problem.

NOTES

1 I will use the terms "small arms and light weapons," "small arms," and "weapons" interchangeably. The most widely accepted UN definition is: *small arms* include revolvers and self-loading pistols, rifles and carbines, assault rifles, and sub-machine and light-machine guns; *light weapons* included hand-held and mounted grenade launchers, portable anti-tank and anti-aircraft guns (and their launchers), recoilless rifles, and mortars of less than 100 mm calibre. *Report of the Panel of Governmental Experts on Small Arms*, United Nations document A/52/298, 27 August 1997, para. 26.

2 For details on the Small Arms Survey see: http://www.smallarmssurvey.org.

3 Rubem César Fernandes, et al., *Brazil: The Arms and the Victims*, forthcoming research report of Viva Rio, ISER and Small Arms Survey, 2005.

4 Ryan Nichols, "Disarming Liberia: Progress and Pitfalls," unpublished paper, 2004.

5 Les Roberts, et al., "Mortality before and after the 2003 Invasion of Iraq: Cluster Sample Survey," *The Lancet* 364 (20 November 2004): 1857–64.

6 This has been publicly reported by the NATO EAPC working group on small arms and landmines.

7 Edward Laurence and Rachel Stohl, "Making Global Public Policy: The Case of Small Arms and Light Weapons," *Occasional Paper 7* (Geneva: Small Arms Survey, December 2002).

8 "Gun Culture in Kosovo: Analysing the roots of belligerence," in *Small Arms Survey 2005: Weapons in War* (Oxford: Oxford University Press, forthcoming 2005).

9 See Fernandes et al.

10 An excellent example of this would be the Organization for Security and Cooperation in Europe's *Handbook of Best Practices on Small Arms and Light Weapons*. See http://www.osce.org/fsc/item_11_13550.html.

LIVING IN DIGNITY

11 FREEDOM FROM FEAR

EFFECTIVE, EFFICIENT, AND
EQUITABLE SECURITY

According to the High-level Panel on Threats, Challenges and Change (HLP), "The maintenance of world peace and security depends importantly on there being a common global understanding, and acceptance, of when the application of force is both legal and legitimate."[1] The provision of security imposes two requirements: those not authorized to use force should renounce its use and threat in their social relations, while the authorized agents of any community with the monopoly on the legitimate use of violence must have the capacity and the will to use force when required. For any international enforcement action to be *efficient*, it must be legitimate; for it to be legitimate, it must be in conformity with international law; for it to conform to international law, it must be consistent with the Charter of the United Nations. For it to be *effective*, it must match resources to mandates and be based on a unity of purpose and action in the international community so as to avoid fracturing the existing consensus. For it to be *equitable*, it must reconcile, or at the very least balance, the competing interests among the many constituencies that make up the international community and avoid privileging the interests and viewpoints of one over the others.[2] To achieve *freedom from fear*, citizens must be assured that national authorities with the legal monopoly of the means of violence will not unleash the agents and instruments of violence on the people, and states must be assured that the most powerful will aim to settle differences of opinion around the negotiating table and not at the point of tank turrets, helicopter gunships, and missiles.

Among the worst acts of domestic criminal behaviour by a government is the large-scale killings of its own people; among the worst acts of international criminal behaviour, to attack and invade another country. The history of the twentieth century was in part a story of a twin-track approach to tame, through a series of normative, legislative, and institutional fetters, both impulses to armed criminality by states, internal and external. Cumulatively and in combination, these attempted to translate an increasingly internationalized human conscience and a growing sense of an international community into a new normative architecture of world order.

In other words, the use of force both domestically and internationally must be tamed and brought under the restraining discipline of the rule of law. But law must also keep pace with the fast-changing security environment. The reality of contemporary threats—for example, a virtual nuclear-weapons capability that can exist inside non-proliferation regimes and be crossed at too short a notice for international organizations to be able to react defensively in time, and non-state actors who are outside the jurisdiction and control of multilateral agreements whose signatories are states—means that significant gaps exist in the legal and institutional framework to combat them. If international institutions cannot cope with today's real threats, states will try to do so themselves, either unilaterally or in company with like-minded allies. Unilateral pre-emption is not permitted under the UN Charter as it is not considered within the acknowledged right of self-defence. But if military action is strategically necessary and morally justified (why should an American president or an Australian prime minister wait for another mass murder, and be prohibited from taking prophylactic action?) but not legally permitted, then the existing framework of laws and rules—not the anticipatory military action—is defective.

The central thrust of this paper will be the growing risks of a separation between lawfulness and legitimacy in the use of force both domestically and internationally and the urgent need to realign them through the concept of the "responsibility to protect." In turn, this cannot be separated from questions of the agency and procedures for authorizing the use of force, the growing gap between law and legitimacy being a function of deficiencies in the structure and workings of such agency and procedures, and thus the need for reforming the structure and operations of the UN Security Council (UNSC) as the core of the international law enforcement system.

For it has signally failed to function so. It was not able to stop either Saddam Hussein's brutalities on his own people or the US war on Iraq. It has been unable to guarantee either Israel's security or the Palestinians' human rights and dignity. In far too many cases, the Security Council has shown itself to be proof against occasions of the larger kind, from Srebrenica to Rwanda and elsewhere. Ineffectual performance has inevitably called into question the credibility of the international organization as the guarantor of world peace and security. But if the Security Council did become more assertive, forceful and effective, its authority would be open to serious question on representational and accountability grounds.

This is why the section of the HLP report dealing with the Security Council is critical for present purposes. As others are taking up the question of Security Council reform, I do not wish to dwell on that in my paper. But I do want to touch on the problem of the veto. The panel acknowledges the veto as being "anachronistic" but sees "no practical way of changing the existing members' veto powers." Accordingly it recommends neither the expansion of the veto to new permanent members under Model A, nor its elimination for the existing five permanent members (P5), although it does recommend a curtailment of the veto's use.[3] If the veto is a genuine contribution to correlating power to responsibility and facilitating the search for great power consensus necessary to international action, it should be held by all permanent members. If it is an obstacle to the effective functioning of the Security Council, it should be abandoned. It seems illogical in any case to have a further differentiation within permanent members under Model A, those with and without the veto.

Of course, the aspiring new members may well in the end agree to this as the price of gaining permanent membership. In that case, we may witness yet another twist in the legality vs. legitimacy debate. During the intense, tense but ultimately futile negotiations over a second Security Council resolution that would have explicitly authorized war against Saddam Hussein, Washington toyed with the idea of claiming legitimacy if it could get 9 affirmative votes (and Japan at least publicly voiced support for such an interpretation), even if the resolution failed due to one or more vetoes. The equation, and therefore the politics, of legality vs. legitimacy is bound to be profoundly affected if there are six more permanent but veto-less members. For the very fact of permanence will enhance their stature and give them continuity, experience, expertise and institutional memory. If the vote on a resolution is 23-1 or 22-2 in a 24-member Council with 11 permanent members, but the resolution is defeated because one of the veto-wielding P5 (V5?) votes negatively, then the gap between legality and legitimacy could become a chasm. If China and Russia were the only two negative votes on a Kosovo- or Darfur-type crisis, and a coalition of the willing went into military action after such an abortive resolution in the Security Council, then it is hard to believe that the coalition would not claim international legitimacy, and would not be conceded to by the international community.

HUMAN SECURITY

Another major explanation for the widening gap between law and legitimacy is the resistance to the emerging new concept of human security and the persistent privileging of national security. Security is an essentially contested concept because it is essentially an intellectual and cognitive construct, not an objective given. In the traditional framework, security is viewed in relation to wars between countries. In order to defend the nation, to pursue national security, many governments have called on citizens to make the ultimate sacrifice. This puts the individual at the service of the state, including killing others and being killed oneself, as and when called for duty by the government of the day. By contrast, human security puts the individual at the centre of the debate, analysis, and policy. He or she is paramount, and the state is a collective instrument to protect human life and enhance human welfare. The fundamental components of human security— the security of *people* against threats to personal safety and life—can be put at risk by external aggression, but also by factors within a country, including "security" forces. The notion of the state as a threat to security is conceptually nonsensical within the traditional paradigm of national security, yet this is in reality the dominant threat to the lives of people from organized violence. Nor can we conceptualize such risks as the earthquake and tsunami of 26 December 2004 within the national security paradigm, even though clearly they should be part of the policy agenda for achieving freedom from fear for large numbers of people. Thus the reformulation of national security into the concept of human security is simple, yet has profound consequences for how we see the world, how we organize our political affairs, how we make choices in public and foreign policy, and how we relate to fellow human beings from many different countries and civilizations.

One "leg" of human security is in the human rights tradition which sees the state as the problem and the source of threats to individual security. The other is in the development agenda that sees the state as the necessary agent for promoting human security. Both are reflected in the UN policy discourse, and indeed may well explain why the human security discourse first arose within the United Nations with the 1994 *Human Development Report* published by the UN Development Programme.

In general, and despite some overlaps as in the Ottawa Treaty banning antipersonnel landmines,[4] Canada and Japan have each emphasized a different leg of human security. Canadians have given priority to protecting citizens at risk of atrocities arising from failed or perpetrator states, and set up an international commission to try to reconcile the imperative to render effective protection to at-risk populations with the persisting reality of state sovereignty. Japan has prioritized the developmental leg of human security, and set up its own World Commission on Human Security to advance this agenda. The Canadian-sponsored commission defined human security as "the security of people—their physical safety, their economic and social well-being, respect for their dignity and worth as human beings, and the protection of their human rights and fundamental freedoms."[5] The Japanese-sponsored commission defined it as protecting "the vital core of all human lives in ways that enhance human freedoms and human fulfilment... It means creating political, social, environmental, economic, military and cultural systems that together give people the building blocks of survival, livelihood and dignity."[6]

The link between the two—the emotional rod that connects both the protection and well-being agendas—is solidarity across borders, the sense of shared affinity with fellow human beings qua human beings regardless of differences in nationality, race, religion or gender. The reality of human insecurity cannot simply be wished away. To many poor people in the world's poorest countries today, the risk of being attacked by terrorists or with weapons of mass destruction is far removed from the pervasive reality of the so-called soft threats that exact a deadly toll every year: hunger, lack of safe drinking water and sanitation, and endemic diseases. These soft threats kill millions every year—far more than the so-called "hard" or "real" threats to security. They are neither unconnected to peace and security, nor can they be ignored until the hard threats have been taken care of. This is why human security can be regarded as a foundational value, from which flow other individual and social values.[7]

This helps too to explain why the African Union has adopted the expansive definition of human security.[8] Africans' security is threatened more by state weakness, incapacity, and absence of effective control over territory, people and resources than by conventional threats of armed attack by other countries. It is also the case that far too many postcolonial African leaderships have ill-served their people and appropriated the resources and power of the state, so that the threat to people's lives has come more from internal repression by one's own state than from external aggression by a foreign state.

At the same time, and recalling the origins of the state in European theory and practice, it is also true that individuals cannot be secure in conditions of anarchy at the state level. The state must be efficient in the provision of law and order and other public goods like basic health and literacy. The best guarantee of human security is a strong, efficient, effective, but also democratically legitimate state that is respectful of citizens' rights and responsive to their needs and concerns, mindful of its obligations and responsibilities to protect their lives and promote their welfare, and tolerant of diversity and dissenting voices.[9] States that are too strong or, at the other end of the spectrum, too weak and failing, cannot provide human security to their citizens. At the same time, states by themselves cannot provide the full measure of human security, but instead must act in partnership with robust market forces and resilient civil society.

Thus secure and stable countries and a body of law that mediates the exercise of power between citizens and the state are prerequisites of human security. But so too is human development, *which is not synonymous with but contributes to human security*, by tackling the long-term structural causes of conflict and by converting the choices available to people from merely theoretical to effective (as in effective demand in economics). Only so can people exercise effective choice to pursue a safe life and livelihood on equal terms with others.

The linkage between the two great agendas of security and development became clearer and more widely accepted after the end of the Cold War. "Peacebuilding" is the bridge that connects the two agendas. It fits far more comfortably under the conceptual umbrella of human than national security. The same is true of conflict prevention: while operational prevention measures aim to mute the prospects of imminent outbreak of violent conflict, structural prevention measures seek to build and consolidate peace through classical development programs promoting state-building, nation-building, economic growth, and reduction of income inequality.

In sum, just as no place on earth resembles the North Pole so much as the South Pole, so freedom from want is the mirror to freedom from fear: the two are not polar opposites.

THE RESPONSIBILITY TO PROTECT (R2P)

At the heart of the international divisions on Iraq in 2003 was not the abhorrent nature of the Saddam Hussein regime, but rather the nature and exercise of American power. Saddam Hussein's record of brutality was a taunting reminder of the distance yet to be traversed before we reach the goal of eradicating domestic state criminality; his ouster and capture by unilateral force of arms was a daunting setback to the effort to outlaw and criminalize war as an instrument of state policy in international affairs.[10]

But what if the second failure is a response to the first, if one country is attacked and invaded in order to halt or prevent atrocities inside its sovereign territory by the "legitimate" government (which already indicates a troubling appropriation and corruption of the word "legitimate")? Who bears the responsibility to protect innocent victims of humanitarian atrocities?

As genocide unfolded in Rwanda in 1994 and 800,000 people were butchered in a mere three months, the world bore silent and distant— very distant—witness to its own apathy. That indifference and inaction by the international community remains one of the most shameful episodes since the Holocaust. This was not a matter of lack of knowledge and awareness, or even of lack of capacity. Rather, it was a failure of collective conscience, of civic courage at the highest and most solemn levels of responsibility.

What if a "coalition of the willing" had been prepared to move in with military force, but the Security Council was deadlocked?

The community-sanctioning authority to settle issues of international peace and security was transferred from the great powers in concert in the nineteenth century to the United Nations in the twentieth century. While Rwanda in 1994 stands as the symbol of international inaction in the face of genocide, Kosovo in 1999 raised many questions about the consequences of action when the international community is divided in the face of a humanitarian tragedy. The NATO intervention in Kosovo in 1999 highlighted a triple policy dilemma of complicity, policy paralysis, or illegality:

- to respect sovereignty all the time is to risk being complicit in humanitarian tragedies sometimes;
- to argue that the UNSC must give its consent to international intervention for humanitarian purposes is to risk policy paralysis by handing over the agenda either to the passivity and apathy of the

Council as a whole, or to the most obstructionist member of the Council, including any one of the five permanent members determined to use the veto clause; and

- to use force without UN authorization is to violate international law and undermine world order based on the centrality of the UN as the custodian of world conscience and the Security Council as the guardian of world peace.

R2P is an important effort to resolve these painful dilemmas. It provides a fresh conceptual template for reconciling both the tension in principle between sovereignty and intervention, and the divergent interests and perspectives in political practice. The topic brings together many of the global trends and evolving norms and state practice with respect to peace and security—the relationship between force and diplomacy, human rights and international security, national security and human security, the United Nations and the United States—and also foreshadows and reflects many of the papers at this conference that focus more directly on UN reforms.

Behind the headlines on the deeply divisive Iraq war was the larger question of the changing nature of threats in the modern world, the inadequacy of existing norms and laws in being able to address such threats, and thus the need for new "rules of the game" to replace them. The United Nations is the arena for collective action, not a forum where nations who are unable to do anything individually should get together to decide that nothing can be done collectively. The urgent task is to devise an institutional framework that can marry prudent anticipatory self-defence against imminent threats to the centuries-old dream of a world where force is put to the service of law that protects the innocent without shielding the criminals.

R2P seeks to do three principal things: change the conceptual language from "humanitarian intervention" to "responsibility to protect," pin the responsibility on state authorities at the national and the UNSC at the international level, and ensure that interventions, when they do take place, are done properly. Because R2P is not an interveners' charter (any more than the Charter of the United Nations is a shield behind which tyrants may torture and kill their own people with total impunity), it does not provide a checklist against which decisions can be made with precision. Political contingencies cannot be fully anticipated in all their glorious complexity and, in the real world, policy choices will always be made on a case-by-case basis. With that in mind, we set out to identify those conscience-shocking situations where the case for international intervention was compelling, and to enhance the prospects of such interventions. In turn, this meant that the circumstances had to be narrow, the bar for intervention high, and the procedural and operational safeguards tight because the probability of international consensus is higher under conditions of due process, due authority and due diligence.

Given the changing nature and victims of armed conflict, the need for clarity, consistency, and reliability in the use of armed force for civilian protection now lies at the heart of the UN's credibility in the maintenance of peace and security. Absent a new consensus and clarity, the UN's performance will be measured against contradictory standards, exposing it to charges of ineffectiveness from some and irrelevance from others, increasing the probability of unauthorized interventions, and further eroding the Security Council's primacy in the realm of peace and security.

Intervention for human protection purposes occurs so that those condemned to die in fear may live in hope instead. It is based in the double belief that the sovereignty of a state has an accompanying responsibility on the part of that state; but that if the state defaults on the responsibility to protect its citizens, then the fallback responsibility to do so must be assumed and discharged by the international community. Thus R2P is more of a linking concept that bridges the divide between the international community and the sovereign state, whereas the language of the right or duty to intervene is inherently more confrontational between the two levels of analysis and policy.

The goal of intervention for human protection purposes is not to wage war on a state in order to destroy it and eliminate its statehood but to protect victims of atrocities inside the state, to embed the protection in reconstituted institutions after the intervention, and then to withdraw all foreign troops. Thus military intervention for human protection purposes takes away the rights flowing from the status of sovereignty, but does not in itself challenge the status. It does supplant the rights of the state to exercise protective functions if the state has proven incapable or unwilling to do so with respect to genocidal killings, humanitarian atrocities, and ethnic cleansing; or to suspend the right of the state to conduct itself free of external interference if such conduct is the cause of the above atrocities. The prevention of the exercise of sovereign rights under intervention for human protection purposes is always limited in time to a temporary period, until the capacity of the state itself to resume its protective functions can be restored and institutionalized.

Intervention for human protection purposes may also be limited in two further respects. It may be confined to a particular portion of the target state's territory rather than all of it, for example Kosovo and not all of Yugoslavia, where the abuses are actually occurring; or it may be limited with respect to a particular group that is the target of abuse, for example Kurds, rather than to all citizens.

The main conclusions of R2P, drawing on the just war tradition, in turn find their way in the HLP report in the form of the five legitimacy criteria: seriousness of threat, proper purpose, last resort, proportional means, and balance of consequences.[11]

WHO DECIDES?

Military intervention, even for humanitarian purposes, is just a nicer way of referring to the use of deadly force on a massive scale. Given the enormous normative presumption against the use of deadly force to settle international quarrels, who has the right to authorize such force? On what basis, for what purpose, and subject to what safeguards and limitations? In other words, even if we agree that military intervention may sometimes be necessary and unavoidable in order to protect innocent people from life-threatening danger by interposing an outside force between actual and apprehended victims and perpetrators, key questions remain about agency, lawfulness, and legitimacy: that is, about international authority that can override national authority.

R2P came down firmly on the side of the central role of the UN as the indispensable font of international authority and the irreplaceable forum for authorizing international military enforcement. What distinguishes rule enforcement by criminal thugs from that by police officers is precisely the principle of legitimacy. The chief contemporary institution for building, consolidating, and using the authority of the international community is the United Nations. It was set up after the Second World War as the framework within which members of the international system could negotiate agreements on the rules of behaviour and the legal norms of proper conduct in order to preserve the society of states. The task therefore is not to find alternatives to the Security Council as a source of authority, but to make it work better than it has.

The legal debate on a clear, consistent, and workable set of codified criteria for intervention is largely sterile. The political debate quickly degenerates from rational discussion to highly charged polemics. Many fear that any codification of the rules of intervention would relegitimize the use of force in international relations. This would be a major step backward, in that over the course of the twentieth century the international community placed increasing legislative and normative fetters on the recourse to military force as a means of settling international disputes.

The response from those with little patience for claims of UN primacy (let alone monopoly) on the legitimate use of international force is that the UN system of collective security was fatally flawed from the start. Peace was preserved and justice advanced by the operation of institutions and the pursuit of values by coalitions of the right-minded, able and willing to defend the international order against all challenges.

The real debate is between those who support the development of guidelines for use by the Security Council in authorizing international intervention but remain firmly opposed to criteria for circumventing the UN, and those who wish to retain the right to unilateral intervention. The first group, comprising mainly (but neither exclusively nor all) of developing countries, is fearful that the norm of non-intervention could become a roadkill on the highway of international power politics.

Among those who wish to retain the flexibility to launch military intervention, if necessary without UN authorization, there is a further division of opinion between those who would like a "doctrine" approach and others who want merely an "exception" approach[12]—a signposted emergency exit from the existing norms as embedded in the UN Charter.

Yet another variation would be to distinguish a "red light" from the entrenched "green light" approach. Under the latter, intervention may not proceed until and unless it has been duly authorized by the Security Council. Under the former, interventions can take place unless and until specifically prohibited by the Council.[13] The difficulty with this is that when the vital interests of major powers are engaged, interventionary forces may go crashing through an entire forest of flashing red lights without paying any heed to them.

Alternatively, it may be argued that the intersection of international law and ethics creates a space where the precautionary principle can be borrowed from environmental ethics and law. Developed especially in Germany and France with regard to environmental law and the legal protection of health, it seeks to provide policy guidance in situations of inherent uncertainty. The precautionary principle states that the absence of certainty must not delay the adoption of measures aimed at preventing the risk of serious and irreversible damage.[14] For if we wait until certainty, irreversible damage may already have occurred. Humanitarian atrocities, genocidal killings, and ethnic cleansing occur against the backdrop of chaos, confusion, and lack of real-time reliable information. If we wait until clarity and certainty obtains, our task may become restitution and retribution, not protection. It should be protection and therefore, in the face of uncertainty, the default bias should be to avoid risk. This is why it is important for the Security Council to deal promptly with any request for authority to intervene where there are allegations of large-scale loss of human life or ethnic cleansing.

CONCLUSION

During the ICISS consultations and study, I was struck by four facts. First, there is a strong consensus among states and in civil society that sovereignty is not an absolute barrier to intervention by the international community in extreme circumstances in order to exercise the responsibility to protect. Second, there is an equally strong consensus that the domestic jurisdiction clause in the UN Charter notwithstanding, Security Council authorization for any intervention is preferable to all other alternatives. Third, in practice, very few states are prepared to insist on and in all cases abide by the principle that Security Council authorization is a necessary precondition for intervention of any type to occur—though there are considerable differences in views about the level of deference that should be shown to the Council. Fourth, despite the clear reluctance to recognize the Security Council as the sole and unique arbiter on all intervention questions, there is nonetheless considerable concern to avoid an outcome that would discredit the Security Council or diminish its authority still further, or that would undermine respect for the principle of an international order based on rules and law rather than simply on power. Thus during the Commission hearings, much of the discussion assumed that calls for intervention would continue to arise and focused on agency, process, and validation issues.

During our worldwide outreach and consultations, nowhere did we find an outright and absolute rejection of intervention in favour of sovereignty. On balance, the desire to avoid another Rwanda (where the world stood by passively during genocide) was more powerful than the desire to avoid another Kosovo (where NATO intervened without UN authorization). Ambassador Colin Keating of New Zealand, president of the Security Council in the fateful month of April 1994, when the Rwanda genocide took place, has added his voice thus: "If the international community is ever to be able to act effectively for human protection purposes, then it must pay attention to the recommendations" of ICISS.[15] Too often in the past UN peace operations have fallen victim to coalitions of the unwilling, unable, and unlikeminded. It is time to put collective might to the service of individual and international right.

How might this be done? What are the next steps? The threefold need is to consolidate evolving norms and practices so that the international community can respond effectively, efficiently, and equitably without undermining the legal order of sovereign states; to establish principles to guide United Nations action; and to establish operational guidelines that hold interventions true to their humanitarian goals. The General Assembly, by means of a resolution or declaration, could revise its interpretation of sovereignty to realign it with accumulated UN practice in the context of humanitarian crises, affirm the civilian protection responsibility of sovereign states and the fallback international responsibility to protect in the extreme cases of state incapacity, unwillingness, or perpetration; and endorse the cautionary principles/legitimacy criteria of grave threat, proper purpose, last resort, proportional means, and balance of consequences. In his recently published report, Kofi Annan makes explicit references to ICISS, R2P, and the HLP, endorses the legitimacy criteria, and urges the Security Council to adopt a resolution "setting out these principles and expressing its intention to be guided by them" when authorizing the use of force. This would "add transparency to its deliberations and make its decisions more likely to be respected, by both Governments and world public opinion."[16]

Our ability and tools to do something beyond our borders, even in some of the most distant spots in the world, have increased tremendously. This has produced a corresponding increase in demands and expectations to do something. An analogy with medicine is appropriate. Rapid advances in medical technology have greatly expanded the range, accuracy, and number of medical interventions. With enhanced capacity and increased tools have come more choices that have to be made, often with accompanying philosophical, ethical, political, and legal dilemmas: the Terri Schiavo case is but the latest tragic example. The idea of simply standing by and letting nature take its course has become less and less acceptable, to the point where in many countries today parents can be held criminally culpable for failure to exercise due diligence in refusing all available treatment for their children.

Similarly, calls for military intervention happen. R2P takes away the last remaining excuses for the international community to sit back and do nothing when confronted with atrocities again. The gap between the need for human protection, sometimes against people's own government, sometimes over the government's objections, and at other times in situations where no functioning government exists, on the one hand; and the ability of outsiders to render effective and timely assistance by lawful means, on the other, has not gone away. Living in a fantasy world is a luxury we cannot afford. In the real world today, the brutal truth is that our choice is not between intervention and non-intervention. Rather, our choice is between ad hoc or rules-based, unilateral or multilateral, and consensual or deeply divisive intervention. If we are going to get any sort of consensus in advance of crises requiring urgent responses, including military intervention, the R2P/HLP principles and legitimacy criteria point the way forward. To interveners, they offer the prospect of more effective results. To potential targets of intervention, they offer the option and comfort of a rules-based system, instead of one based solely on might. To all sides, they offer the possibility of efficient, effective, and equitable security.

Instead of the position of being the "nattering nawabs of international negativism," therefore, those developing countries who wish to resist undue encroachments on sovereignty and major powers who wish to retain the maximum freedom of action in the unilateral use of force should engage constructively in the shaping of the new norms. Establishing agreed principles to guide the use of force to protect civilians under threat will make it more difficult, not less, to appropriate the humanitarian label to self-serving interventions while simultaneously making the Security Council more responsive to the security needs of civilians. The challenge is neither to deny the reality of intervention nor to denounce it, but to manage it for the better, so that human security is enhanced, the international system is strengthened, and all of us come out of it better, with our common humanity not diminished but enhanced.

NOTES

1 *A More Secure World: Our Shared Responsibility.* Report of the High-level Panel on Threats, Challenges and Change (New York: United Nations, document A/59/565, 2 December 2004), para. 184.

2 Some commentators, while agreeing with the need "to combine power with principle," nonetheless believe that the HLP report "ends up bowing more to the raw distribution of power than to international principles." Satish Kumar, "Global threats and U.N. reforms," *The Hindu* (Chennai), 24 March 2005.

3 HLP, para. 256.

4 See Ramesh Thakur and William Maley, "The Ottawa Convention on Landmines: A Landmark Humanitarian Treaty in Arms Control?" *Global Governance* 5, 3 (July–September 1999): 273–302.

5 *The Responsibility to Protect: Report of the International Commission on Intervention and State Sovereignty* (Ottawa: International Development Research Centre for ICISS, 2001), 15. I was one of the ICISS Commissioners and indeed one of the principal authors of its report.

6 *Human Security Now* (New York: Commission on Human Security, 2003), 4.

7 Hans van Ginkel and Edward Newman, "In Quest of 'Human Security,'" *Japan Review of International Affairs* 14, 1 (Spring 2000): 59–82.

8 See Jakkie Cilliers, *Human Security in Africa: A Conceptual Framework for Review* (Pretoria: African Human Security Initiative, 2004), 8.

9 See Simon Chesterman, Michael Ignatieff, and Ramesh Thakur, eds., *Making States Work: State Failure and the Crisis of Governance* (Tokyo: United Nations University Press, 2005).

10 Elizabeth Wilmshurst, the former deputy legal adviser to the British Foreign Office, resigned from her post on the eve of the Iraq war because, she wrote in her letter of resignation, military action in Iraq was "an unlawful use of force" which "amounts to the crime of aggression"; *BBC News,* 24 March 2005, downloaded from http://news.bbc.co.uk/2/hi/uk_news/politics/4377469.stm.

11 HLP, para. 207.

12 For a review of this debate, see in particular Simon Chesterman, *Just War or Just Peace? Humanitarian Intervention and International Law,* (Oxford: Oxford University Press, 2001), 226–32, and Nicholas Wheeler, *Saving Strangers: Humanitarian Intervention in International Society,* (Oxford: Oxford University Press, 2000), 33–51. For updated discussions on the subject more generally, see also J. L. Holzgrefe and Robert O. Keohane, eds., *Humanitarian Intervention: Ethical, Legal and Political Dilemmas* (New York: Cambridge University Press, 2003); and Jennifer M. Welsh, ed., *Humanitarian Intervention and International Relations* (Oxford: Oxford University Press, 2004).

13 This is reminiscent of the secret to the professor of comparative jurisprudence during the Cold War. There are only four root systems, he said; once you have grasped that, you can master all the different variations. In Britain, everything is permitted unless specifically prohibited in law; in Germany,

all is proscribed unless specifically permitted in law; in the Soviet Union all is permitted in law but banned in practice; and in France everything is prohibited in law but permitted in practice.

14 See David Freestone and Ellen Hey, eds., *The Precautionary Principle and International Law: The Challenge of Implementation* (London: Kluwer Law International, 1996); James Cameron, "The Precautionary Principle," in Gary P. Sampson and W. Bradnee Chambers, eds., *Trade, Environment, and the Millennium*, 2nd ed. (Tokyo: United Nations University Press, 2002), 287–319.

15 Colin Keating, "Rwanda: An Insider's Account," in David M. Malone, ed. *The UN Security Council: From the Cold War to the 21st Century* (Boulder: Lynne Rienner, 2004), 510.

16 Kofi Annan, *In Larger Freedom: Towards Development, Security and Human Rights for All*. Report of the Secretary General (New York: United Nations, document A/59/2005, 21 March 2005), paras. 122–35.

12 THE UN REFORM AGENDA AND HUMAN RIGHTS

I am deeply honoured to address such a distinguished group this evening of Ambassadors, UN professionals, and scholars, all quite obviously committed to improving the United Nations, as was evident today from the extremely rich and often quite heated discussion that we had throughout the day.

I'm also pleased this evening to be joined by so many Canadians, because Canada has played a critical, perhaps even a unique, role in contributing to and promoting the effectiveness of the United Nations. I wish there were more Canadas out there. We need more governments and more people with such a profound commitment to the United Nations.

I also want to recognize several members of the Human Rights Watch Toronto Committee who are here this evening. I'm very proud that Toronto is one of our most vigorous and active committees around the world.

I speak this evening at a moment of enormous opportunity for the United Nations. As many of you know, there have been recent reports on UN reform issued by the High-level Panel that Kofi Annan appointed, as well as by the Secretary General himself. These reports tried to identify the major problems facing the global organization and to outline some of the possible solutions.

I'm particularly happy, given that my role here is to discuss human rights, that many of these recommendations reflect Kofi Annan's profound personal commitment to integrating human rights into the broad mandate of the organization—his recognition that everything from security to development is furthered by a genuine commitment to human rights, and thus that the broad purposes of the United Nations are advanced by this commitment.

My focus this evening, as Ambassador Allan Rock mentioned, is the problem of the UN Human Rights Commission and the proposed solution to that problem in the creation of a new Human Rights Council.

But before I address that issue, I'd like to highlight four other human rights ideas that have emerged from these two recent reports— ideas that I think deserve to be promoted and implemented.

First, and I have to begin with this, given that I am here in Canada, is the renewed endorsement of the idea of the "responsibility to protect" people who are facing mass atrocities.

This is an idea that originated in Canada. It's an idea that has been pushed by Canada. And it's an idea that I'm very happy to see is being broadly embraced by the international community. Our challenge now is to move beyond the idea stage, because as I speak there are massive atrocities still taking place in Darfur. I'm quite pleased that the Security Council last week was able to approve several resolutions, including a historic referral of the situation in Darfur to the International Criminal Court, but none of us can afford to be complacent because we are not yet exercising our "responsibility to protect" the people of Darfur. To this day, the African Union still has not gotten its act together to deploy the 3,000 peacekeepers that have been authorized, and that force does not even have a clear protection mandate. And there is no one I can see who is volunteering to provide additional troops.

It's clear that it is not going to be enough to simply rely on the African Union. It's doing a good job with the handful of troops that it has there. But some combination of African Union pride and Security Council indifference (or indifference on the part of the rest of the world) is precluding the deployment of a substantial peacekeeping force in Western Sudan comparable to the force that was just authorized for Southern Sudan. And that is a deployment that is urgently needed—one that if we believe in the "responsibility to protect," we must make sure happens very, very quickly.

Second, I was pleased that the UN reform reports took on the issue of military intervention for humanitarian purposes. And here I want to highlight the effort to define the conditions in which military intervention is appropriate to save lives.

In particular, it is suggested that such military intervention should be limited to cases in which there is actual or imminent large-scale killing. That's a line that I believe in. It's one that, we should be clear, means that the Iraq war cannot be justified as a humanitarian intervention, because even though one clearly could have justified invading Iraq, say, in 1988, at the time that Saddam was committing genocide against the Kurds and killing 100,000 of them. Or you could have justified intervention in 1991 when he was murdering 30,000 uprisers among the Shia and the Kurds. There simply was no mass slaughter of that sort taking place in March 2003. And so if we can't justify the war as one to seize Saddam's supposed but non-existent weapons of mass destruction, and if we can't justify the war as one to stop Saddam's supposed but non-existent links with terrorists, we also can't justify it as a humanitarian intervention. That's the logical implication of the criteria set out in these reports.

And it's one that is important because we shouldn't forget the fact that, first of all, since war involves killing people, it should be reserved, if it's to be justified in humanitarian terms, for situations in which there is a genuine humanitarian crisis—a massive loss of life.

Second, as we have now seen, Darfur being the illustration, humanitarian intervention is a finite resource. A large part of the reason it is so difficult to find international troops for Darfur is because so many of the potential contributors are preoccupied in Iraq, or parallel to that, in Afghanistan. And so I think to a large degree the people of Darfur are paying a price for what in my view was a misguided humanitarian intervention, a non-humanitarian intervention, in Iraq.

And of course we saw this in our conversation today. People are very nervous. They're anxious about legitimizing the idea of humanitarian intervention for fear that they're going to authorize future Iraqs. I fear that if we allow that war to be justified in humanitarian terms, we risk discrediting an institution that is needed by people in Darfur-like situations.

Now a third issue emerging from these reports that I wanted to highlight has to do with the use of the veto on the Security Council. There was much discussion today about whether the Security Council should be expanded and how many new permanent members should be provided. Whatever the answer you arrive at to those questions, the fact remains that perhaps the most important thing that could be done from a human rights perspective in terms of improving the functioning of the Security Council would be to implement the recommendation coming out of these reports that the veto not be used in situations where there were mass atrocities at stake.

The veto was designed to be exercised when one of the five permanent members had an acute national interest at stake, and I think it's fair to say that it is extraordinarily rare, perhaps never the case, that such an interest arises in a situation of mass atrocities.

I don't expect this to become a formal rule because the current permanent members wouldn't allow it, but it would be wonderful if this became an informal norm and a clear practice. I hope the governmental representatives here will push for that development.

The final point I'd like to address before I turn to the issue of the Commission is the definition of terrorism that has emerged from these two reports. And here, quite simply, the clear statement that there is never a justification for terrorism is extraordinarily important—that no war of national liberation, nothing, regardless of the justice of your cause, justifies deliberately killing civilians. That is an important statement, and its importance is augmented by the fact that it was endorsed by Amre Moussa, a member of the High-level Panel, who has made clear that he was acting in that respect not simply in his personal capacity but as the Secretary General of the Arab League. If indeed that definition can be formalized into law, it would be a huge step forward.

Now I wish that the parallel problem of state terrorism had not been neglected. The excuse was given that because we have international humanitarian law, we don't need to deal with state terrorism. But that isn't true because humanitarian law only applies in war situations, and we all know that state terrorism can happen even in what technically might be a time of peace. But leaving aside that fault, it would be enormously important if this emerging consensus were solidified into a treaty making clear that there is never a justification for attacking civilians.

Let me turn to the Commission itself. I don't need here to repeat the litany of embarrassments that are often cited by those who want to discredit the Commission, and thereby the UN as a whole. One points to the fact that Libya was the Chair of the Commission, that Sudan is today a member of the Commission, that Cuba plays a prominent role on the Commission. These are the kinds of attributes that are difficult to justify.

How did this happen? To a large degree the Human Rights Commission has become a victim of its own success. If you look back twenty, thirty years, the Commission didn't do much of anything. Because it never condemned governments, it didn't matter much and therefore was largely ignored. But over the last twenty years, as it has begun to condemn governments for their gross abuses of human rights, those governments have found that its stigma is quite sharp. It's something to be avoided at all costs.

And so they have decided that the best way to avoid being condemned is to join the Commission and try to defeat its condemnations from inside. We have thus seen, particularly over the last decade, a flocking to the Commission by governments who are not there to promote human rights but are there to undermine any effort to enforce human rights. It has gotten to the point that roughly half of the 53 members of the Commission today are there simply to defeat the purposes of the Commission.

They vote against almost any country resolution unless Israel is the target. They vote in favour of so-called no action motions which are basically censorship motions that preclude even discussion of human rights problems in particular countries. They're constantly proposing reforms which seek to undermine the various special rapporteurs and investigators that report on their human rights abuses.

And often they succeed. Occasionally the human rights community is able to get a country resolution through the Commission, but it's an uphill battle. More often than not, countries that should be condemned are ignored. The Commission has become an "Abusers' Defence Society" rather than an institution to protect human rights.

Now the blame for this lies in part with the regional blocs, because the way Commission membership is determined is that each bloc selects a number of candidates according to the number of seats it is allocated. And what has become the norm is that, let's say, Africa is allocated twelve seats, so it will propose exactly twelve candidates—a so-called clean slate. That means the rest of the world has no opportunity to influence the African membership, that it basically must ratify the selection of the regional bloc

And it's not just Africa. Other regions including the Western group do the same thing. In fact, when the Western group didn't offer a clean slate and the United States was voted off the Commission, the Western group changed its practices. And so now virtually everybody puts forward a clean slate, and the global vote for Commission members is largely meaningless. It has become a ratification of the selections already done by the regional blocs. And many regional blocs pay very little attention to the human rights credentials of the candidates they put forward.

Other problems with the Commission have to do with the fact that it meets only six weeks a year during one marathon session in March and April. There's one going on right now in Geneva. What this means is that there is at best perfunctory consideration of the reports of the various investigative rapporteurs. There is little or no opportunity to follow up on recommendations or resolutions passed last year. There is little opportunity to respond to an emergency, unless the emergency happens to fall in that six-week period. While technically an emergency session can be called, it hardly ever happens. So if you happen to show up in, say, June with a genocide, you're told sorry, come back in March. That's hardly a way to play an effective preventive role.

Now this amalgamation of problems is not only undermining the UN's leading political body in the human rights realm. It's hurting the reputation of the United Nations as a whole. This is not just a human rights problem, this is a United Nations problem. That's why the UN Human Rights Commission was given such prominence in the two recent reports.

What is the solution to this problem? Well, the High-level Panel largely shared the diagnosis that I have just described to you, but when it came to prescription, it chickened out. It couldn't achieve a consensus on the kind of reform that would really change things and so instead it basically threw in the towel. It said, well, we can't figure out a way consistent with UN traditions to impose human rights criteria for Commission members, so instead let's just open the Commission up to everybody. Let's invite all 191 members of the United Nations to join the Commission. Create a second General Assembly.

Is that a good idea? Well, first of all it would basically preclude the idea of a body that meets year-round. For all practical purposes, that becomes logistically impossible when you're dealing with so many governments. Second, it essentially gives in to the abusive governments and says, you can continue to be the judge for your own misconduct. And third, the General Assembly itself doesn't do very well. If you look at the most recent meeting of the General Assembly, it adopted censorship motions, those so-called no-action motions, and didn't even discuss, let alone criticize, atrocities in Darfur, Belarus, and Zimbabwe. The General Assembly actually had a worse record this past year than the Commission. So I don't think that throwing in the towel and adopting universalization of membership is the answer.

Kofi Annan had much more courageous recommendations. He has put forward the idea of creating a Human Rights Council. This is an idea that I very much endorse. But the question comes up, why would a smaller Council, people talk about twenty-five or so, why would that not just replicate the membership problems of the Commission?

As my concluding remarks, let me try to offer some answers to that question. First, there are a couple of improvements that we could take whether we stick with the Commission or go to the Council.

We need to begin to pay attention to the process of selecting candidates to whatever body it is. This is a decision that, as I mentioned, is made by the regional blocs and largely operates under the radar screen. I don't think any government at the meeting of its regional bloc feels that it's going to pay any political price for putting forward a highly abusive government. Nobody holds them responsible.

So one thing we can do is to begin to treat this candidate selection process as a serious political decision. This should be a matter of bilateral discussion.

Friends of human rights should actively solicit good candidates from all regions. Some smaller countries might be very committed to human rights but lack the financial wherewithal to mount the sort of enlarged mission that would be needed in Geneva. For those governments, a trust fund should be created from which they could draw to create an enlarged mission to handle human rights work, particularly for a year-round Council as Kofi Annan has proposed. So these are the kinds of things that I think would elevate the candidate selection process and make it better.

Second, there's been much talk about the idea of introducing criteria for membership. This is something that Human Rights Watch has been actively discussing and promoting for a number of years. In response, we have heard that there's no way in the UN context that governments are going to impose criteria on themselves. And we accept that there are certain political limitations here.

So more recently we've been putting forward a softer alternative— the idea that anybody who wants to be a member, whether it's of the Commission or the proposed new Council, should have to make a human rights pledge. This would not be binding, but it would at least demonstrate a commitment to the purposes of the Commission or Council.

Now what would such a pledge look like? There are various possibilities, but it could include, for example, a pledge to complete ratification of all the major human rights treaties. It could involve a pledge to complete reporting under those treaties. It could involve issuing a standing invitation, an open invitation, to UN human rights investigators to come and look at a government's country whenever they wanted. It could include adopting a Human Rights Action Plan for your own country, such as recommended by the 1993 World Conference on Human Rights, which would set forth how a government plans to improve human rights at home. It could involve pledges as to how a government will vote in the Commission or Council—a pledge to vote consistent with the purposes of promoting human rights. And it should certainly include a pledge not to vote in favour of these censorship "no-action" motions on any country resolution.

I'm sure you can think of other possible pledges as well. Introducing these pledges would allow us to begin a virtuous competition, a competition to raise the bar, rather than a race to the bottom, as has often been the case with the secretive, closed regional bloc selection process that exists so far.

Now, having mentioned improvements that could be made in either the Commission or the Council, there are a few reasons why the Council would be better than the Commission.

First of all, the Council as I mention, would be a year-round body. That would allow it the time needed to seriously consider a country's situations—to become really expert and to consider country situations over time, rather than give it the perfunctory treatment that currently is often the case in Geneva. It would allow time for follow-up, and one of the things that I've learned after these many years in the human rights field is that you don't get any place without follow-up. If you do one-shot human rights work, you may as well go home. To get something done, you've got to stick with it over time, and the Commission is not able to do that during its compressed six-week period. A permanent Council could.

And obviously, a permanent Council could play an emergency role. When your genocide breaks out, it's there, ready to act. Indeed, it could anticipate the genocide and begin to play the preventive role that we all like to talk about but is so difficult to achieve within the United Nations.

Finally, and perhaps most important, the way I think you can make a huge difference on the membership front is in the rules for voting on Council members. The biggest problem, as I mentioned, is those clean slates which essentially deprive most of the international community of any say on who the members are from anywhere other than your own regional bloc.

Kofi Annan has proposed that to be a member of the new proposed Council, you would have to attract two thirds of the vote of the General Assembly. That's a good idea, but I would take it a step further.

In allocating membership on the Council, you obviously have to allocate a certain number of seats to each region, but I would leave a number of at-large seats as well. That would undermine the incentive of regions to present clean slates, because if they presented a clean slate, they would have to accept the minimum regional representation. They would effectively opt out of competing for any of the at-large seats—something that few if any regions would presumably want to do.

To claim the at-large seats, a region would have to put forward a slate that was larger than the minimum for its region—that is, not a clean slate. And to secure the votes of two-thirds of the General Assembly for those candidates, all of the candidates would have to be reasonably attractive in human rights terms. That would have a tendency to raise the calibre of the candidates.

This is roughly the procedure used by the Assembly of State Parties to choose the judges for the International Criminal Court. I would look to that voting procedure as a model to be used in ensuring that the Human Rights Council does not just replicate the Commission.

Let me end by noting that this is not and should not be a North-South issue. I know that there's some effort to turn it into one, but that is wrong. Many, many southern governments today are strong defenders of human rights, and indeed we know that some northern governments are major human rights problems.

We also know that southern governments have perhaps the greatest interest in an effective United Nations, and we have seen that we will not have an effective United Nations if its leading political body on human rights continues to be an embarrassment. This should be a major priority for coalitions like the Human Security Network, the Community of Democracies, and, frankly, any international body that has the welfare of ordinary people as a part of its mandate.

The UN has played a leading role over the decades in setting international human rights standards. What we desperately need today is reform on the issue of implementation. Failure to take the courageous steps that Kofi Annan has outlined risks not only undermining the standards that the UN should be upholding, but also undermining the UN itself. That we cannot afford.

INSTITUTIONAL INNOVATION

EDWARD C. LUCK

13 THE UN SECURITY COUNCIL
REFORM OR ENLARGE?

The Secretary General's sweeping reform plan[1] has many impressive attributes: its conceptual teaming of development, security, and human rights; its bold proposal for a smaller Human Rights Council populated, no less, than with member states that actually respect the rights of their citizens; its timely suggestion for a Peacebuilding Commission; and its unambiguous strategy for defeating global terrorism. Unfortunately, however, it is weakest where it should be strongest: in its diagnosis and prescriptions for the Security Council. If this were a routine report of little or no consequence, then even an academic as hyper-critical as this one would be prone to look away and to ascribe the report's tortured reasoning and unsupported conclusions about the Council to rushed drafting and inattention from the thirty-eighth floor. But the Secretary General has staked the Organization's future— as well as his own—on this plan, initially claiming that this vision must be adopted in its entirety, swallowing the bad ideas along with the good.

Never before has a Secretary General sought to put his personal stamp so firmly on the restructuring of the UN's—and arguably the world's—premier inter-government political body. It is territory on which his predecessors were wise not to tread. The report's discussion of the Security Council is flawed in its history, diagnosis, and prescription. These shortcomings could seriously undermine the whole reform process given the Secretary General's mistaken assertion that his package be treated as the kind of grand bargain that has failed to materialize in past reform campaigns. The three sets of concerns will be addressed here briefly in turn.

FAULTY HISTORY

The report implies that the Council has lost its way over the years and needs to be restored to its founding concept, when actually it is just beginning to realize some of that initial promise. Oddly, the Secretary General posits that the Charter created three Councils—for security, for social and economic affairs, and for trusteeship—more or less on a par, but that the security one "has increasingly asserted its authority and, especially since the end of the Cold War, has enjoyed greater unity of purpose among its permanent members."[2] Therefore, he concludes, "we need to restore the balance."[3] This turns San Francisco on its head. The whole point was to have the permanent members work together so that the Security Council could, indeed, be assertive. And did not the Secretary General launch his drive for "radical reform" in September 2003 for just the opposite reason, i.e., that the permanent members were deeply divided over whether to use force in Iraq? Moreover, did anyone at San Francisco believe that the three Councils should or would be "balanced" in their influence and impact? If so, why was the Security Council given powers that were without precedent either in the UN system or in human history?

The report echoes the common wisdom that the Security Council needs to be "more representative of the international community as a whole, as well as of the geopolitical realities of today."[4] This assertion has been repeated so often by so many in the UN community that no one asks anymore why the Charter failed to use terms like "representative" or "democratic" to describe any organ, much less the Security Council. True, a number of smaller or southern delegations at San Francisco wanted a larger and more equitable Security Council and sharply questioned the inequities of permanent membership and the veto power for some. The convening powers, however, would not countenance any of this, for their greatest concern was to avoid replicating the shortcomings of the League of Nations' Council: equal rights, consensus rules, and a membership that reached its greatest girth (and irrelevance) in the mid-1930s, on the eve of World War II. They explicitly rejected the notion that the Security Council should be representative, democratic, or equitable.

True, times have changed much more than the Council has. But those claiming that its composition and procedures need to be radically altered should acknowledge that they are seeking to reverse the founding conception, not to restore it. They also need to do a much better job of explaining why they believe the Council has failed and why their remedies will foster positive change. The Secretary General and his High-level Panel properly underline the advantages of articulating criteria for Council membership that would fulfill the reference in Article 23(1) to a candidate's "contribution ... to the maintenance of international peace and security." Yet this, too, was debated at some length in San Francisco and it was decided to forego all of the criteria proposed by various delegations in favour of a loose formulation that would permit political factors to be taken into account. The selection of the five permanent members, undertaken by the US, UK, and USSR prior to San Francisco, was not on the basis that they were the world's most powerful countries—France and China at that point would not have fit that description—but because they were the leading allies in the war against fascism. At that point, the UN was an alliance not an incipient universal organization.

Yes, the Council has outpaced the other larger and more representative organs, but this would seem to confirm the founders' contention that smaller is sometimes better. The Secretary General's report could have productively devoted more attention to why the other, supposedly more "democratic" bodies, have done so poorly rather than calling for the Security Council to follow their path. The advocates of this course should tell us which UN intergovernmental bodies became stronger and more effective as their composition grew. And why does the Secretary General tell us that the Human Rights Commission needs to shrink to become more viable and credible, while the Security Council needs to grow?

FAULTY DIAGNOSIS

Undoubtedly there is growing pressure from many quarters for expanding the Council. The aspirants for permanent membership are in the vanguard of the movement, of course, but the sentiment that the Council's composition is "anachronistic or insufficiently representative," to use the Secretary General's phrase,[5] is widespread. According to a recent cross-national survey, this may be true among peoples as well as governments.[6] Political popularity, however, is not sufficient grounds for radically transforming the one UN organ that arguably functions reasonably well. Ironically, the very pressure for expansion testifies to the equally prevalent impression that serving on the Council has political and psychic benefits, as it is the one UN body that is believed to have real clout at times. No such rush to join ECOSOC, especially after its two enlargements, has been detected. Like brain or heart surgery, the downside risks of unnecessary or misdirected surgery on the Council could be very high, even fatal. Yes, we would all like sharper brains and stronger hearts, but we are understandably reluctant to embark on such surgery unless we are convinced both that we would die otherwise and that the results are very likely to bring a marked improvement in our condition. The diagnosis, under such a scenario, should be unambiguous and compelling. One does not volunteer for such an operation for marginal or uncertain gains.

In terms of the health of the Security Council, the Secretary General and his High-level Panel essentially have given us a three-part diagnosis: 1) that the Security Council is in poor, even terminal, condition; 2) that its legitimacy and credibility are low and declining; and, as noted earlier, 3) that there are some new geopolitical and power realities that demand a fresh set of actors around the Council table. On the first piece of the diagnosis, it is worth noting that the General Assembly's never-ending Working Group on Council reform commenced its deliberations a dozen years ago, when the Council was reaching its peak in terms of activity, whether measured in terms of resolutions, statements, or blue-helmeted peacekeepers deployed, and with no veto having been cast in the previous three years. That pace has, with some ups and downs along the way, largely been maintained since. Indeed, it is likely that more peacekeepers will be deployed under Council mandates next year than ever before. With an expanding array of subsidiary bodies devoted to countering terrorism and a growing appetite for addressing thematic issues, the most frequent complaint—echoed, as noted above, in the Secretary General's report— concerns the Council's hyperactivity, not passivity.

In calling for radical reform in September 2003, following the inability of the Security Council's members to agree on a course of action in Iraq, the Secretary General seemed to be claiming that the Council's problems were institutional rather than political. If so, he appears, to this author at least, to have misdiagnosed the ailment. Would a twenty-four-member Council have been any more likely to have produced consensus over Iraq? Or would President Bush, instead, simply have been less likely to have gone to the larger Council in the first place for further authorization to use force? Reform follows political convergence, not the other way around. By putting the cart before the horse in seeking radical reform before the political wounds over the use of force in Iraq could heal, the Secretary General increased the risk not only of falling short on reform but also of exacerbating political tensions among the member states. His overly dramatic rhetoric about a severe institutional crisis now threatens to become a self-fulfilling prophecy.

At his press conference on the release of the report, the Secretary General asserted that the proposed enlargement would make "the Council more democratic and more representative, and thus it will gain greater legitimacy with those decisions."[7] The report, on the other hand, underlines that the reform must make the Council "not only more representative but also more able and willing to take action when action is needed."[8] The Secretary General's report, like that of the High-level Panel before it, acknowledges that legitimacy comes from efficiency and effectiveness as much, or more, than from equity. Both reports endorse the "responsibility to protect" doctrine and, seemingly, a more proactive, interventionist stance by the Council in cases of egregious mistreatment of a population. Yet two of the four aspirants for permanent seats under Model A—Brazil and India—have been outspoken opponents of just such humanitarian interventions, while the other two aspirants—Germany and Japan—have political or constitutional constraints concerning participation in such operations. Would the addition of more members, especially permanent ones, broaden the scope and impetus for Council action? Or, as this author believes, would it actually result in having a greater chance that one member or another would object to intervening in any given crisis? Composition may well be one component of authority and legitimacy, but most surely it is not the only one.

More puzzling are the repeated references to "the geopolitical realities of today,"[9] to "the realities of power in today's world."[10] What "realities" does the Secretary General have in mind? Unfortunately, he never says. Presumably he is not referring to the trend toward unipolarity in military affairs, as the US has emerged as the only member state with global military reach. Even in economic matters, the US has two-and-a-half times the GDP of the next largest economy, Japan. With raw or hard power more concentrated, why should the number of permanent members be more than doubled? The High-level Panel made similarly vague and ill-defined references to new power realities as a rationale for Council expansion. Without further explanation of the assumptions and calculations that produced it, this conclusion will ring hollow and, to this author at least, unconvincing. For it sounds as if these plans for expansion seek not to reflect power realities but to deny and counter them.

FAULTY PRESCRIPTIONS

Is the Security Council such a well-crafted instrument that it need not be touched by the tides of reform? Of course not; its flaws are manifold. Processes of renovation and renewal should be ongoing, year after year, as an integral part of the life of the Council, as well as of the UN's other principal organs. But simply adding seats to a flawed enterprise does nothing to improve the way it relates to other organs or reaches out to the larger UN membership. A few more countries are to be pulled into the charmed circle, but nothing is to be done to make it any more representative of the concerns and interests of the rest of the membership. There is nothing in these models about consulting with other member states, whether regionally or globally. Nothing is said about accountability or transparency, about reporting to the Assembly, or about assessing whether bold Council resolutions were ever followed-up with bold actions. Nothing is said about how sanctions regimes could be monitored more closely in the future to avoid future Oil-for-Food scandals.

Neither the High-level Panel nor the Secretary General display much concern about how the enlarged Council would go about its work or about how the new members would act once they attain permanent status. Their preoccupation, instead, is with the size of the body. Without the former, i.e., without first tackling working methods, no real reform is being proposed at all; certainly nothing that would faintly qualify as radical, bold, or imaginative. The UN has been down this road before, when the Council was expanded in the mid-1960s. While initially opposing the enlargement, the permanent members accepted it in the end. In part this no doubt reflected Cold War politics and a recognition of the rapid expansion of UN membership, especially from Africa and Asia, with decolonization. But the permanent members also came to appreciate that, without parallel changes in working methods, they would still dominate an expanded Council. The same is true today, only under Model A there would be a wider circle of large states with little incentive to modify working methods.

This suggests an initial parallel focus on two critical questions: 1) reforming working methods to enhance accountability and transparency, building on the useful first steps achieved over the past decade and 2) exploring ways of ensuring that the members of the Council, new or old, permanent or elected, make more of an effort to be representative, whether through consultative processes, explanation of votes, or interactions with troop contributors, donors, and countries affected by conflicts in their neighbourhood or region.[11] Being from a region does not make a Council member representative of its neighbours or others in its region. Indeed, the principal stumbling blocks to efforts to enlarge the Council in the past stem from deep divisions within regions, and the same is true today. While there is no basis for regional seats in the Charter and proposals along those lines were turned aside at San Francisco, it is hard to conceive of any way to handle the question of representation in a body of 191 sovereign member states without employing some sort of regional model. The Assembly recognized this principle in its earliest decisions regarding the organization of its work, even with less than one-third of the current membership and no reference to regional groups in the Charter.

In the meantime, the advocates of expansion, particularly of permanent seats, could usefully clarify several points that are not addressed in the two reports or are not consistent between them.

- First, neither report indicates how many affirmative votes would be required for decisions on either procedural or non-procedural matters in the proposed twenty-four-member Council. Would it be 14, 15, or 16? Where this hurdle is set would significantly affect the degree of influence of individual elected members, the political dynamics within the Council, and how readily and quickly it could respond to urgent developments affecting peace and security.
- Second, the High-level Panel called for a review conference in 2020 of the Council's composition and the contributions of the members to the Council's effectiveness.[12] The Secretary General's report makes no reference to such an event. Why was this dropped? Some of the aspirants for permanent seats had intimated that the review mechanism would mean that their performance would be more accountable than that of the five with the permanent-for-life seats of 1945. The Secretary General's proposals, therefore, sound less innovative and less concerned with accountability than were those put forward by the Panel.
- Third, neither report seems to envision much of a place on the Council for smaller member states or even the middle powers that have meant so much to peacekeeping, humanitarian affairs, and human rights over the years. Both the proposed criteria for membership and the structure for the Council's categories for members, whether under Model A or B, are premised on the assumption that the Council should be populated with as many large states as possible. There is a logic to this, of course, but it would

be hard to sustain the argument that historically small and medium powers have been responsible for the Council's failings. They have, moreover, a major stake in the success of collective security arrangements because they often face security threats that they are unable to handle on their own. The large majority of member states, of course, fall into these categories and, from what many of them tell me, their opportunities to serve on the Council would come with even less frequency under either Model A or B.

The two reports fail, as well, to cite any historic cases in which a larger Council would have responded differently. It is fine to assert in the abstract that an expanded Council would make better decisions or bring more resources to bear in implementing them, but it is hard to identify a case when this would have been so in practice. As noted before, there is every reason to expect that a Council of twenty-four would be just as divided as one of fifteen over Iraq. How adding permanent members philosophically opposed to the doctrine of a "responsibility to protect" would make the Council more likely to intervene in Darfur, Democratic Republic of the Congo, or Rwanda escapes this author.

The criteria for membership proposed by the two reports seek to reward those member states already assisting the collective effort importantly in terms of financial or troop contributions. On one level, this seems fair and makes good sense. But on another level, if the proposed permanent members are already making major contributions without such seats, why would they either be in a position to contribute much more or have an incentive to do so once they gain permanent status? In terms of fairness, in other words, the criteria are attractive, but the companion argument that adding the new permanent members would produce substantial new resources for collective action seems overly optimistic.

Finally, and most critically, the timing of this drive for Council expansion seems both unpropitious and unfortunate. The politics among the member states, as well as the Secretary General's weakened position in the midst of the Oil-for-Food revelations, suggest that the chances of developing a broad-based consensus on the Secretary General's package are low to poor. When this author worked with Razali Ismail on his proposed Council reform in 1996–97, the political atmosphere looked a good deal more promising. More than 120 member states had indicated privately their willingness to support the Razali plan, but few chose to endorse it publicly when he courageously launched it in the never-ending Working Group in the Spring of 1997.

Wisely, the new Secretary General, Kofi Annan, at that point did not tie his own management reform proposals to the fate of the plan for the Security Council. Much of his July 1997 plan was implemented—at least those aspects that did not depend on intergovernmental approval—and the Council did adopt some initial reforms in its working methods. Now, however, that lesson in the value of de-linking distinct aspects of a complex reform package seems to have been lost. If the member states are faced with a take-it-or-leave-it package, there is little doubt at this point that they would choose the latter. Instead, the most likely pattern—as always—is for the Secretary General to propose and the Assembly to dispose. Parts of the package will be adopted, parts will be modified, and much will be left for further deliberation down the road. My guess is that Council expansion will, once again, be relegated to the third option.

In my view, that would not be a bad outcome. The UN's chief challenge relates not to the size of the Council table but to its uneasy relations with Washington, DC and with American power. Understandably, the delicate yet decisive question of relating multilateral expectations to the unipolar concentration of military capacity is not addressed frontally in either report. But the Secretary General's references to new power realities, both reports' insistence on a much larger Council, and the Secretary General's apparent preference for Model A and more permanent members—clearly on display at his 21 March 2005 press conference—all suggest an intention to try to dilute American influence within the Council. That perception is certainly prevalent in Washington, DC, where many see this as the unstated sub-text for this drive to enlarge the Council. The fact that the Secretary General launched his personal campaign for "radical reform" in the wake of the use of force in Iraq certainly speaks to this interpretation.

For the many in the secretariat and among the member states who had hoped that the Council would serve as a counter-weight to Washington's power and penchant to use force, the vision of counterbalancing US hard power with the soft power of larger voting majorities in an enlarged Council must be quite seductive. Unfortunately, it would be a self-destructive path not only for the Council, but for the world body as a whole. The UN was created, in part, to harness American power and determination to a multilateral framework and agenda. The founders were determined not to leave the US out of the new enterprise and not to repeat the League's failures. Relations between the US and the UN, never easy, are going through a particularly rough patch at the moment. Each side needs time to sort through the implications of the new power realities that have left the US as the world's only super-power. One element that needs further thought is the role of the Council vis-à-vis American power. Like working methods, this should be addressed before deciding who ought to sit around the table. For those member states that have long pressed for permanent membership, further delay would certainly be frustrating. But it beats putting the whole enterprise at risk at the time when it can least afford further divisions and unfulfilled expectations. For those who say they care the most about the institution, the choice should be easy.

NOTES

1 Report of the Secretary General, *In Larger Freedom: Towards Development, Security, and Human Rights for All*, A/59/2005, 21 March 2005.
2 *In Larger Freedom*, para. 165.
3 *In Larger Freedom*, para. 166.
4 *In Larger Freedom*, para. 168.
5 *In Larger Freedom*, para. 165.
6 The order and wording of the questions, however, may have influenced the outcome. BBC World Service Poll, "23-Country Poll Finds Support for Dramatic Changes at UN," http://www.pipa.org/OnlineReports/BBCworld-poll/030505/html/bbcpoll3.html.
7 SG/SM/9772, 21 March 2005.
8 *In Larger Freedom*, para. 168.
9 *In Larger Freedom*, para. 168.
10 *In Larger Freedom*, para 169.
11 These points, and some of the earlier ones, are explored at greater length in Edward C. Luck, "Rediscovering the Security Council: The High-level Panel and Beyond," in Ernesto Zedillo, ed., *Reforming the United Nations for Peace and Security* (New Haven, CT: Yale Center for the Study of Globalization, 2005), 126–52.
12 United Nations, *A More Secure World: Our Shared Responsibility*, Report of the Secretary General's High-level Panel on Threats, Challenges, and Change (New York: United Nations, 2004), para. 255.

14 WORKING BETTER TOGETHER
IMPLEMENTING THE HIGH-LEVEL PANEL'S
RECOMMENDATIONS ON PEACEBUILDING

I

In its analysis of the United Nations capacity to promote and maintain peace, the Secretary General's High-level Panel on Threats, Challenges and Change identified

> a key institutional gap: there is no place in the United Nations system explicitly designed to avoid State collapse and the slide to war or to assist countries in their transition from war to peace. That this was not included in the Charter of the United Nations is no surprise since the work of the United Nations in largely internal conflicts is fairly recent. But today, in an era when dozens of States are under stress of recovering from conflict, there is a clear international obligation to assist States in developing their capacity to perform their sovereign functions effectively and responsibly....Strengthening the United Nations capacity for peacebuilding in the widest sense must be a priority for the organization.[1]

There is by now ample evidence of substantial gaps in the planning, financing, and implementation capacities for the critical civilian components of complex missions. While substantial improvements have been made over the years in the international community's peacebuilding capacities, concepts, policies, and practice continue to evolve within the UN system, including the international financial institutions, and among bilateral donors. In proposing the creation of a Peacebuilding Commission and related Peacebuilding Support Office (PBSO) in the Secretariat, the High-level Panel (HLP) is seeking to build on and consolidate these advances in order to strengthen national as well as the UN's and international community's shared capacity to prevent state failure and more effectively manage post-conflict peacebuilding.

The Peacebuilding Commission (together with the PBSO) is intended to create an authoritative, intergovernmental mechanism that can make the substantive link between diplomatic, security, and development functions and ensure that for each specific country situation a comprehensive, integrated mission plan is followed, that there is adequate coordination among the diverse intergovernmental and national donor agencies, and that sufficient resources are marshalled to ensure that the bases for sustainable peace and development are put in place. How to make this work in practice is the subject of this chapter.

II

Consistent with the HLP's focus on the centrality of responsible and effective states to ensure peace and security, there has been increased attention in recent years to institutional frameworks for setting policy and delivering outcomes, both among donor nations and in intergovernmental organizations. Various UN departments, programs and specialized agencies have worked hard to develop their individual civilian response capacities, as have the Bretton Woods institutions, and some regional organizations.[2] Recognizing their own civilian response shortcomings, bilateral donors, most evidently the United Kingdom and the United States, have developed their own national-level policy planning and coordinating bodies to more effectively address issues of post-conflict recovery and peacebuilding, and to these same ends other European donors are seeking ways to build flexibility into their funding lines for relief and development.

These efforts at national-level coordination and resource mobilization are milestones in the recognition of the importance of engaging fully and effectively in conflict management and post-conflict peacebuilding. However, they also signal the additional importance of developing an effective international or intergovernmental mechanism, such as the HLP's proposed Peacebuilding Commission and the Peacebuilding Support Office at the UN, for at least two reasons.

First, there is a clear need to increase coverage beyond the limited capacities of individual governments or intergovernmental organizations (IGOs). By most counts, more than fifty civil wars have been terminated since 1989;[3] yet, the UN-mounted, Security Council-mandated peacebuilding operations in only twenty-one, or less than half of these, as well as in Afghanistan and East Timor, and the US was involved in less than one-third, not counting Afghanistan and Iraq. Moreover, over the past five years, there has been an average of fifteen conflicts occurring concurrently, with US aspirations limited to addressing at best two to three of these simultaneously. Under these circumstances, the vast majority of post-conflict cases will continue to fall into the category of forgotten or neglected crises with increased risk of a reversion to conflict. Given the mobility of global terrorism, weapons of mass destruction and organized crime, triage among these pockets of instability will not provide a certain enough safeguard against these threats to international peace and security.

Secondly, even in those situations that the international community decides to act, there is a risk that increased national capacities among a few better endowed or motivated countries, conflated with national interest calculi and impatience with less agile or competent partners, will lead to further fragmentation in the international response, resulting in a possibly more robust but partial and uncoordinated response that will be less effective than a strategically calibrated one. Competing mandates and interests have plagued post-conflict reconstruction efforts in the past, with agencies butting heads in the pursuit of roles and resources and governments seeking to "brand" projects that might justify expenditures to their citizens. Even as individual governments and IGOs seek to improve their performance, there is an undeniable need to pull together the diverse national and intergovernmental efforts to maximize the individual capacities of cooperating agencies; to reduce redundancies and competition and establish an effective division of labour; and to marshal sufficient resources to get the job done in a timely manner. The much maligned word, "coordination" aside, there is mounting evidence that multilateral cooperation and burden-sharing produce better outcomes.

III

The UN has a critical role to play in this regard, in part because of the particular comparative advantage it brings to the table. Its universal membership, impartiality, and multinational staff provide it with a degree of legitimacy and credibility unmatched by any regional organization, the Bretton Woods institutions, or bilateral donors. Moreover, in the course of the past quarter-century, the UN has gathered considerable experience and expertise in post-conflict recovery and reconstruction, often through reflection on its own shortcomings and failings. Finally, as James Dobbins has pointed out in his recent assessment of the post-conflict effectiveness of the UN and the United States, the

UN has performed rather remarkably well in extremely difficult circumstances. Dobbins attributes success to seven out of eight UN-led cases and only four out of eight US-led cases, despite the fact that UN operations tend to be understaffed and under-resourced. To quote Dobbins,

> Assuming adequate consensus among Security Council members on the purpose for any intervention, the United Nations provides the most suitable institutional framework for most nation-building missions, one with a comparatively low cost structure, a comparatively high success rate, and the greatest degree of international legitimacy.[4]

IV

These relative assessments notwithstanding, UN capacity is extremely incomplete and uneven.[5] Despite advances made by unifying its field presence in a single "house," by the establishment of country teams, and by the deployment of integrated missions, the effectiveness of the UN response to complex crises continues to be weakened by incoherent and overlapping planning and funding appeals, and by competing mandates and agendas of multiple agencies and programs. For its part, the Security Council sets mission mandates on a somewhat myopic basis—normally six months to a year—with a focus on political settlement and elections as the precondition for early exit, often leaving unattended the conditions that gave rise to conflict in the first place. There is little consultation with the development side of the system, either with the programs and agencies, including the UN Development Group (UNDG), with the international financial institutions (IFIs), or with non-governmental organizations (NGOs), let alone with donor government development or finance ministries. The donors themselves often fail to coordinate, and sometimes disagree on, the political objectives at hand and the strategies for achieving them. And, there is continued lack of funding for the essential state-building functions that need to occur within the first year to eighteen months of peacebuilding. The proposed Peacebuilding Commission, Peacebuilding Support Office and Peacebuilding Fund represent innovative and promising mechanisms to address these problems.

V

While there appears to be growing consensus about the need for a more effective mechanism for post-conflict reconstruction and peacebuilding, the guidelines laid out by the High-level Panel raise a number of critical questions about form, function and decision-making authority that must be resolved before any decisive action on the Peacebuilding Commission and associated Peacebuilding Support Office can be taken.

In brief, the High-level Panel recommends that:

The Peacebuilding Commission should be reasonably small; it should meet in different configurations, to consider both general policy issues and country-by-country strategies; it should be chaired for at least one year …by a member approved by the Security Council; in addition to representation from the Security Council it should include representation from the Economic and Social Council; national representatives of the country under consideration should be invited to attend; the Managing Director of the International Monetary Fund, the President of the World Bank and, when appropriate, heads of the regional development banks should be represented at its meetings by appropriate senior officials; representatives of the principal donor countries and, when appropriate, the principal troop contributors should be invited to participate in its deliberations; and representatives of regional and subregional organizations should be invited to . participate in its deliberations when such organizations are actively involved in the country in question.[6]

Elsewhere, I have laid out the implementation issues that need to be resolved by member states in the run up to the forthcoming Summit at which it is hoped that agreement can be reached on establishing the Peacebuilding Commission and endorsing the Secretary General's plans for a Peacebuilding Support Office in the Secretariat.[7] In this chapter, I want to argue four basic points: 1) function should determine form; 2) field vs. headquarters capacity and coordination is a false choice; 3) the funding gap must be finally closed; and 4) the debate on institutional locus can be resolved on substantive grounds.

FUNCTION SHOULD DETERMINE FORM

In his note to the General Assembly transmitting the report of the High-level Panel, the Secretary General endorses the Panel's recommendation to establish a Peacebuilding Commission, and states that:

work and resources in this area remain too dispersed and I welcome the idea of a new intergovernmental body, as well as that of dedicated capacity in the Secretariat. It is my hope that such a Commission, which would assist states in the transition from the immediate post-conflict phase to longer-term reconstruction and development, would also be available, at their request, to assist member states in strengthening their own capacity.[8]

As described in the Panel's report, the Peacebuilding Commission is intended to enhance the security-bound planning, implementation and monitoring capacity of the Security Council/Secretariat, by ensuring simultaneity of critical peacebuilding tasks. By bringing together members of the Security Council, ECOSOC, the IFIs, and major donors, it would help to link at headquarters the diplomatic, security, and development dimensions of complex missions, thereby providing greater support capacity for field operations. It would enable the Security Council to draw in a consistent and systematic way on the knowledge, experience and resources of the World Bank and the International Monetary Fund, as well as the development ministries of member states, all present in the field but not readily a part of Security Council deliberations.

In his own March 2005 report (drawing on the HLP), the Secretary General states that the

> Peacebuilding Commission could perform the following functions: in the immediate aftermath of war, improve United Nations planning for sustained recovery, focusing on early efforts to establish the necessary institutions; help to ensure predictable financing for early recovery activities, in part by providing an overview of assessed, voluntary and standing funding mechanisms; improve the coordination of the many post-conflict activities of the United Nations funds, programmes and agencies; provide a forum in which the United Nations, major bilateral donors, troop contributors, relevant regional actors and organizations, the international financial institutions and the national or transitional Government of the country concerned can share information about their respective post-conflict recovery strategies, in the interests of greater coherence; periodically review progress towards medium-term recovery goals; and extend the period of political attention to post-conflict recovery.[9]

Beyond these process functions, and implicit in both reports, is the explicit end-goal of any post-conflict reconstruction or peacebuilding effort: to wit, the restoration or development of effective and legitimate public institutions capable of exercising control over the legitimate use of force and providing essential goods and services to the populations that live within their defined borders.[10] The Peacebuilding Commission needs to be constituted with this goal and the expertise necessary to achieve it firmly in mind.

There are a host of "to do" lists associated with post-conflict reconstruction and peacebuilding. However, these tend to be task-oriented rather than strategically-driven and need to be prioritized and sequenced to the demands and realities of the particular post-conflict and political circumstances.[11] Defining the required civilian skills and resources in technical categories related to reconstruction and peace-building—infrastructure, transitional security, rule of law, humanitar-ian assistance, and economic development—misses the analytical framework and integrated approach to statebuilding that provides the only real basis for longer-term stability. Concepts such as governance and participation get us closer to that goal, but the approach is usually limited to "strengthening civil society" and holding elections. Build-ing legitimate and effective institutions for public administration, man-agement and finance, are essential to winning public trust and avert-ing (a return to) conflict. Multiple actors with relevant competencies are essential to getting this right.

These functions pertain by-and-large to instances of post-conflict reconstruction and peacebuilding, leaving open the critical question of the role to be played by the Peacebuilding Commission with regard to prevention and, in particular, countries at risk, a role initially envi-sioned by the High-level Panel. In his transmittal letter conveying the Panel's report to the General Assembly, the Secretary General recog-nized that the wherewithal to help build capacity in post-conflict coun-tries could have dual use for conflict prevention, but stipulated that this should be at the request of the countries in question. In his recently released supplemental report, he sharpens his view, stating:

> I do not believe such a body should have an early warning or monitoring function, but it would be valuable if member states could at any stage make use of the Peacebuilding Commission's advice and could request assistance from a standing fund for peacebuilding to build their domes-tic institutions for reducing conflict, including through strengthening the rule of law institutions.[12]

While this should successfully elide some states' concerns regarding sovereignty and intervention by asserting the responsive nature of the Peacebuilding Commission's role in conflict prevention, consid-erably more thought needs to be given to the means and methods of addressing the needs of fragile states and questions of impending state failure.

FIELD VS. HEADQUARTERS CAPACITY AND COORDINATION IS A FALSE CHOICE

There is no question but that conflict prevention and post-conflict peacebuilding need to be field-driven and consistent with national goals and aspirations if they are to have any traction. However, significant back-up support at headquarters is essential to the success of any field mission. There appears to be general recognition of the need for an authoritative body to guide policy, set standards, bring development and security together with the politics of the moment, share experiences and best practices among diverse actors, maintain a sustained focus on post-conflict requirements, provide coherence in specific country cases, oversee and monitor progress in transition strategies and operations, flag problems, marshal resources, and track commitments and disbursements.

Reflecting the need for both a strong field orientation and comprehensive back-up, the Peacebuilding Commission should consist of a core group and country (or region) specific sub-groups based on an organizing principle of variable geometry. As stipulated by the Secretary General in his March 2005 report, the composition of the core group must be shaped in relation to its ability to provide coordination and advice of sufficient scope and magnitude to define a peacebuilding strategy and devise general policies and procedures. It therefore should include representation from the UN system as a whole, including the Security Council, ECOSOC, bilateral donors, and major troop contributors, as well as by senior officials of the World Bank and the International Monetary Fund. Although not stipulated in the Panel's report or subsequent documents, additional consideration should be given—at the discretion of the Secretary General—to representation by the UN funds and programmes, perhaps through participation by the Chair of the UNDG.

To accommodate the issues of appropriate participation, effective size, and legitimacy, it would be important to supplement the Commission's core group, charged with the general tasks of policy and oversight previously described, with sub-groups that could be convened, possibly within the region or affected country itself, to attend to specific country situations on a case-by-case basis. Participation in these sub-groups, or committees, should consist of: senior representation from the country under consideration; the SRSG or his/her senior designee for peacebuilding and coordination; senior officials of relevant regional and sub-regional organizations; regional actors involved in the peacebuilding strategy, as appropriate; country directors of the World Bank and IMF and a senior official of the relevant regional development bank; representatives of major donors to that country, and troop contributing countries. These country specific sub-groups should liaise closely with civil society actors in the transition countries.

A number of recommendations have been put forward regarding the means of selecting membership and participation in both core and sub-groups, and I will not attempt to summarize or advocate for any of them here. Each requires trade-offs between size and breadth of participation which in turn have consequences with respect to institutional politics and questions of legitimacy. Whatever selection criteria are ultimately chosen, however, two things need to be kept clearly in mind. First, representation and membership are different forms of participation and carry with them implications for quality of participation and decision making. Secondly, and closely related, is the need to distinguish between legitimacy that is derived from participation and the legitimacy that is derived from effective results.[13]

To be truly effective, the Peacebuilding Commission would need to be accompanied by concomitant reforms within the Secretariat, as clearly identified in the HLP recommendation to create a Peacebuilding Support Office. As previously noted, there is a definite need to address the current state of competence and capacity within the UN, both in terms of human resources and organizational structure by bringing together experienced and specialized staff who are now dispersed throughout the system, in an institutional arrangement that provides one-stop shopping for analysis, planning and support for peacebuilding missions. As in the case of the Commission, the Peacebuilding Support Office would provide a support function to the field, initially working closely with the UN country team to lay the groundwork for the SRSG or Special Representative. It would also work in close cooperation with the Department of Peacekeeping Operations (DPKO) (normally the lead planning department) to provide coordinated backstopping at headquarters for ongoing field operations, including advice on best practices, access to technical expertise through maintenance of rosters in essential areas of peacebuilding, and serve as a resource for the Peacebuilding Commission.

YES, THERE IS A FUNDING GAP THAT MUST FINALLY BE CLOSED

The High-level Panel recommended the establishment of a $250 million Peacebuilding Fund to ensure adequate and timely funding of the essential civilian components of a lasting and sustainable peace. While the modalities for the use of funds and for its replenishment need to be negotiated, there is general agreement that timely and predictable funding is needed for: a) the costs of early recovery and rehabilitation, b) financing essential public sector activities until self-sustaining revenues can be generated, and c) initial economic pump-priming, including job recovery and agricultural production, until mainstream development financing and private sector investment come on board.[14] There is also accumulating evidence that the economic costs of internal conflict make an ounce of prevention more than worth a pound of cure.[15]

For more than a decade now, efforts have been made to address the well-documented relief to development gap in post-conflict financing. In an effort to close that gap, a number of donor countries have built flexibility into their accounts for humanitarian assistance and development; the Compliance Assistance Program (CAP) has been extended; UNDP has established both the Trust Fund of the Bureau for Crisis Prevention and Recovery (BCPR) as well as country-specific trust funds; and the World Bank has created a Post-Conflict Fund, following on its experimentation with the Holst Fund for recurring cost of the Palestine Authority. In some cases, such as that of East Timor, the Security Council included some additional activities as part of assessed funding. These innovative efforts notwithstanding, serious gaps continue to hamper efforts at reintegration of former combatants and displaced persons, training and deployment of indigenous police forces, judicial reform, recurrent costs of fledgling government services, and other essential civil institution-building elements of peacebuilding.

In his March 2005 report, the Secretary General suggests that one role for the Peacebuilding Commission would be to help "ensure predictable financing for early recovery activities, in part by providing an overview of assessed, voluntary and standing funding mechanisms."[16] While there is compelling reason to front load these essential national capacity-building activities in post-conflict countries, it is unlikely that many of them will ever become part of assessed budgets, as in the case of the "DD" but not the "R" of disarmament, demobilization and reintegration. Moreover, others would argue that there is a certain risk in securitizing the entire peacebuilding enterprise. Still, as in the Albright corollary to the Powell doctrine for the overwhelming use of force, it is reasonable to ask what good is it to have the system in place to devise comprehensive strategies if you cannot pay for their implementation?

Presuming that the argument for the creation of a Peacebuilding Fund is now compelling, a number of issues remain to be decided, including modalities for its establishment, replenishment, and use. The Fund could be set up either as a standing fund to be replenished on a periodic basis by willing donors, as a revolving fund to be used as an advance account to be repaid as pledges for country activities are realized, or as a draw-down facility whose pre-pledged funds would be released upon approval by the Peacebuilding Commission of a plan of action based on a joint, field-based assessment. In either case, the Peacebuilding Commission should have authority over country allocations based on an acceptable, field-derived coherent plan of action. Peacebuilding funds should be put as quickly as possible at the disposal of field operations, either directly through the SRSG, the Resident Coordinator or, where there is sufficient confidence, national authorities as a first demonstration of their capacity to deliver public goods and services.[17] At the very least, procedures for accessing trust funds held at headquarters need to be streamlined. Under any scenario, a system for full accountability from recipients as well as from donors needs to accompany the establishment of any funding mechanism.

THE DEBATE ON INSTITUTIONAL LOCUS CAN BE RESOLVED ON SUBSTANTIVE GROUNDS

The High-level Panel has recommended that the Peacebuilding Commission be established as a subsidiary body of the Security Council, after consultation with ECOSOC, thereby raising a set of questions about the relationship between the two bodies. In his March 2005 report, the Secretary General notes that the Peacebuilding Commission "...would best combine efficiency with legitimacy if it were to report to the Security Council and the Economic and Social Council in sequence, depending on the phase of the conflict. Simultaneous reporting lines should be avoided because they will create duplication and confusion."[18]

While fully agreeing with the point of simultaneous reporting, I would urge that we substitute "state of recovery" for "phase of conflict." If we can agree that restoring or building legitimate and effective state institutions is the sine-qua-non of successful peacebuilding then we should be able to agree to front load those components that are necessary corollaries of peace and security into Security Council mission mandates. When public institutions are again operating normally and able to provide for public safety, security and well-being in an atmosphere of relative peace, ECOSOC would be able to assume its role consistent with the Charter's allocation of responsibilities as between competent bodies. The Peacebuilding Commission, comprised of members of both the Security Council and ECOSOC would provide for appropriate consultation in the restoration of those public functions.

A number of additional considerations argue for a first association with the Security Council, including: the political weight and
authority afforded by the Security Council; the simultaneity needed
between peacekeeping and peacebuilding operations; the required
coordination across phases of conflict—prevention, mediation, peacekeeping and peacebuilding; and the need to inform security considerations with longer-term development goals. The economic and social
bodies in the UN system have perspectives, expertise, experience, and
resources that need to be included from the outset in fashioning, implementing and monitoring comprehensive post-conflict peacebuilding
strategies that for their part must become a central part of the definition of peace and security.

VI

The international community has been working its way incrementally
toward the establishment of a Peacebuilding Commission since the
UN became seized with post-conflict reconstruction and recovery
nearly two decades ago. The process has had its fits and starts, but
the logic of the outcome has been clear for some time. Obviously, the
idea of the Peacebuilding Commission is itself not the answer to the tra-
vails of building sustained peace and development through effective,
legitimate and accountable states. It is necessary to get the functions,
structures, and decision-making rules right, and it is essential that the
human resource capacity and financial wherewithal be firmly in place.
The High-level Panel Report has provided a much-needed catalyst to
the process of reforming not simply the United Nations but the way in
which the broader international community—donors, IFIs, regional
organizations, NGOs—organizes itself to ensure that fragile states do
not slide into conflict and that states in conflict recover sufficiently to
manage their own sustainable peace. The Secretary General's March
2005 report takes us one step further toward implementation of three
unassailable recommendations: the creation of a Peacebuilding Commission, a Peacebuilding Support Office within the Secretariat, and a
Peacebuilding Fund. We must not squander this opportunity to work
better together to prevent conflict and restore peace.

NOTES

1 United Nations, *A More Secure World: Our Shared Responsibility*, Report of
   the High-level Panel on Threats, Challenges and Change, December 2004, 83.

2 See Forman, et al., papers prepared for the Copenhagen Conference on Civilian Crisis Management, June 8–9, 2004, at www.cic.nyu.edu/publications.

3 Charles Call uses this measure in his recent review of peacebuilding concepts and capacities for DPA.

4 James Dobbins et al., *The UN's Role in Nation-Building: From the Congo to Iraq* (New York: Rand, 2005), xxxvii.

5 This is true throughout the system. See aforementioned Copenhagen papers for a detailed assessment of the civilian response capacities of the UN Secretariat, the specialized agencies and programmes, the IFIs, and the EU.

6 United Nations, *A More Secure World: Our Shared Responsibility*, Report of the Secretary General's High-level Panel on Threats, Challenges, and Change (New York: United Nations, 2004), 84.

7 See Discussion Paper on the High-level Panel on Threats, Challenges and Change "Recommendation to Establish a Peacebuilding Commission", prepared for the January 17, 2005 meeting hosted by the Governments of Denmark and Tanzania.

8 HLP, 3.

9 HLP, 32-3.

10 In his March report, *In Larger Freedom: toward development, security and human rights for all*," the Secretary General notes that "'The proposals...are designed to strengthen States and enable them to serve their peoples better by working together on the basis of shared principles and priorities... one of the great challenges of th new millennium is to ensure that all States are strong enough to meet the many challenges they face." UN Document A/59/2005, 6.

11 In an unpublished paper, "Building Institutions After Conflict," Sarah Cliffe and Nick Manning, of the World Bank, cite public safety and security, rule of law, economic planning and public finance management, and service delivery as the first order of business.

12 *In Larger Freedom*, para. 115.

13 In *Power and Governance in a Partially Globalized World*, Keohane posits that legitimacy has two components and that international institutions are judged both on the procedures they follow (inputs) and on the results they obtain (outputs). Robert Keohane, *Power and Governance in a Partially Globalized World* (London: Routledge, 2002), 234.

14 The timeframe for "gap" funding is variably considered to be between 6-18 months.

15 See Paul Collier, unpublished paper, c. 2005.

16 *In Larger Freedom*, 31.

17 Note Collier's point that national public expenditures for military are not best use of aid which is better apportioned for purposes of economic growth.

18 *In Larger Freedom*, para. 116.

MOBILIZING ACTION

15 MAKING THE CASE FOR CHANGE

Thank you. I welcome the chance to be here. We have one useful practice at the University of Winnipeg that is relevant to these proceedings— the "brown bag lunch" series where students and faculty can get together to harass the president while munching on sandwiches and celery sticks.

The tone is not one of highbrow challenges to higher education, but the pragmatics of how to keep tuition low, subsidized parking for the faculty, and a good basketball team for the alumni. It is the academic equivalent of question period.

So when Paul asked me to re-emerge from the Academy for a brief fling into the rarefied world of policy discussion, I thought a brown bag approach might be relevant–examining the politics and pragmatics of UN reform—the "how to," not the "why," and drawing upon my days as a political practitioner whose job it was to figure out the way to translate good ideas into action. And with apologies to our guests from other countries I want to focus those considerations fundamentally on the role Canada can play in fostering reform because I believe an effective UN is in our interest and we have a vocation to play in helping to make the change.

It is with some pride that I can say that I come from a country that has a solid history of endorsing the UN. Even in the dark days of suspicion surrounding the Iraq imbroglio, close to 60 percent of Canadians, when polled, thought the UN made a difference in world peace and security. When compared to the average global range of ten to twelve percent, it paints a picture of the level of commitment Canadians feel for this organization. It is a commitment tinged with a questing, a questioning of what needs to be done in order for the UN to remain the effective governing body it has been, and of the steps we must take to ensure its continued guiding presence in this ever-changing world of global politics.

One thing I learned in politics is that there's nothing more challenging than trying to get politicians to change their own institution. Turkeys do not vote for Christmas.

As a foreign minister I was basically a plumber, fixing leaks. But, I recognized that the leaks were more frequent when the architecture was faulty. Post-Berlin Wall, most accustomed assumptions were challenged, and there was to be a New World Order. By the mid-1990s the bloom was off and everyone was looking for the right compass setting. It was that need for navigation that took us into the realm of ideas because everything else didn't seem to work. And the first task was simply to recognize how difficult it is to make changes and institute reform.

I am reminded of a talk by the great Canadian economist Harold Innis. He gave a presidential address to the Royal Society in 1948 called Minerva's Owl. Minerva's Owl only flies at dusk with the light of day behind it. Innis took this to mean that by the time we have become aware that calamity is upon us it is already too late to take action; that we recognize important signs of issues still to come too late to respond. As a result we fall back on old answers or react out of haste, lack of forethought, and inattention. Or we simply get caught flat-footed.

A more academic example of this can be found in the writings of the American philosopher of science Thomas Kuhn. Kuhn argues that paradigmatic shifts of thinking occur with great resistance and only after a point of crisis has been reached. He offers the Copernican and Galilean helio-centric vs. geo-centric model of the solar system as an example of the human rigid adherence to established conceptual norms. Kuhn observed, "Novelty emerges only with difficulty, manifested by resistance, against a background provided by expectation." Eventually even the most resilient had to cede in the face of ever mounting evidence to our place in the galaxy.

It is only after a tremendous amount of dissonance in response to new cognitions that change begins to take form. According to Kuhn, a shift of paradigm cannot grow from the last, but rather supplants it with a whole new set of cognitions. In that sense a new paradigm cannot grow out of the faulty foundation of the one it replaces. Reform cannot be achieved by an "à-la-carte" method of keeping the old and supplementing with the new. It calls for a complete revamping of existing institutions, structure, practice, convention, and assumption, which are showing signs of losing relevance in the face of this new global reality that we are facing.

In this country, we are on the cusp of such a paradigmatic shift of thought. The post-Cold War, post-Berlin Wall global situation is one that presents a new set of challenges and requires a new set of approaches. We are dealing with a whole new range of issues that are affecting the Canadian populace, from employment issues to the new global face of health (one need look no further than the SARS outbreak to realize that matters of health are no longer just a national concern) to the foreign policy issues that are reflecting an increasingly borderless world.

That is the issue facing reform. Incremental changes, the fixing of small leaks will just not suffice. The question is what happens if effective multilateralism is no longer capable of managing what we now see are major global issues. Multilateralism is still steeped in the nation-state, which forms the foundation of the United Nations, which in turn lays the foundation of our international government system. The question which must be considered is: Is the UN capable of looking outside of itself to sense this impeding shift of global consciousness? As the Jesuit theologian Teilhard de Chardin wrote, "a great many internal and external portents—political and social upheaval, moral and religious unease—have caused us all to feel more or less confusedly that something tremendous is taking place in the world." But, what is it?

I think you at least have to carry into this period of change in determining whether, if you wouldn't mind my using a baseball analogy, whether you hit a Bobby Thomson home run as we did in 1951, that changed the entire stream of what happened in baseball, or if in fact are you a New York Yankee which just builds up a like a machine, steadily rolling on. Are we going to try implementing great change in small increments? Or do we need what David Malone called the big bang. I call it the home run.

Implicit in the UN reform document is a fundamental paradigmatic change. If one were to analyze the basic elements of the report, it would underline the argument that I am making here today. We are living in a time of global concerns, of large issues which will require a global-mindedness in their resolution.

The threats to human security we are facing today are not the threats of old which could be contained within national borders. Climate change, disease, poverty, terrorism, are but a few examples of the types of challenges we face today, challenges which will not be kept at bay by increased border security or greater military force.

Can I give you one example? Back in 2000, we sponsored in Winnipeg a big conference looking at the issue of war-affected children. In recent discussion with representatives from our downtown school division in Winnipeg, it was brought to my attention that nearly four thousand of these war-affected children can be found right in the heart of Winnipeg. That's four thousand potentially traumatized children in Winnipeg alone. This is no longer an issue of helping African children in some far-off corner of the globe. It is an issue of helping Canadian children deal with the trauma that they've experienced prior to arriving on our doorstep.

When faced with these types of realizations one cannot help but begin to comprehend the shifting of cognition, from one of national identity to one of global citizenship. I have little doubt this shift of paradigm is taking place, as was so devastatingly evidenced by the tsunami that hit South Asia this past December.

This tragedy and the response that ensued was not handled by unilateral or bilateral means. It took a global outpouring of sympathy and financial aid, which incidentally started not with governments but with individuals. This is an example of what American political scientist Richard Falk has called "globalization from below." It was the enormous expression of public opinion that drove that response that ultimately came from governments. We've established that there is a shift of consciousness that will necessitate change and reform but the vital question is "Will the decision makers take notice?"

In following topical events this last while, I was struck by the realization that the question of the hour may not just be how to implement reform, but how to get the world to pay attention to the change, and the need for change. Among the countless articles on Terry Schiavo, Michael Jackson, and Pope John Paul II's illness, I was challenged to find meaningful media coverage addressing the proposed reform of the UN. Where there was coverage it was on the Volcker Report and the image erosion caused from the Oil-for-Food imbroglio. It is hard to mount a campaign for reform when the public mind is centred on spicy dollops of scandals.

But I believe there is an appetite for change. And it is my belief that there is a public appetite to search beyond the conventional wisdoms and trite routine explanations to find some answers on how to reconcile a world divided by borders but faced with global issues.

At last count, there were over 25,000 human rights organizations around the world. The co-operative and cohesive voice of that number of people demands notice. Through the tools of international communication and organization, we are approaching a time when the new global "superpower" might well be comprised of multinational corporations and NGOs. We are witnessing the birth of a new type of civil society, a civil society mobilizing on a international level to ensure the continued existence of a global public domain, a public domain that will stand up to governance that it sees as being detrimental to the greater public good.

It is this organized force that will drive the policy decisions that must be made, decisions such as setting specific criteria for inclusion to the Human Rights Council, such as abstaining from the veto in cases of humanitarian disaster. Unless the will of the people is reflected in the decision making, than can we really call it reform?

We are on the cusp of a paradigmatic political shift. The digital revolution of the last twenty years has greatly enhanced the effectiveness of civil society. We are at the dawn of the day where individual groups, NGOs, will organize themselves to wield ever increasing influence on legal and political policy. The informational innovations that have come into being over the last fifteen years or so have greatly empowered the citizens of the world to share information and to mobilize action on an international level. I can think of no better example to offer than the tremendous role that the NGO community played in the signing of the Ottawa Treaty. Decision makers must open the doors of the fortress to that community and engage them in dialogue. Civil society in turn must continue to lobby decision makers for the change they wish to see in the world. Unfortunately, the UN has not really been good at this point in time about how to deal with "civil society" or global citizenship.

The reform package does not adequately address the role of civil society, allotting only a few sentences of the report to the critical role that civil society has come to play in furthering humanitarian causes. This change is upon us and it is one, which I believe, is here to stay.

This new political force can play the role of catalyst, of a spark to begin mobilizing for change on such vital issues as human rights, economic development, AIDS, disease, the environment, peace and disarmament just to name a few. There's an untapped potential of political power that can be mobilized in implementing reform. All that is required is focus and direction.

As Canadians, we are all aware that there is an appetite for reform that more closely reflects our values, our humanitarian sensibilities. *The Responsibility to Protect* was borne out of this appetite. The new report centres on this idea of the "responsibility to protect."

But in order to achieve this goal some fundamental changes must occur within the very structure of the governing body to which we look to implement it. There must be greater transparency and accountability involved in the decision-making process at every level. If the UN is to remain relevant as a global governing body, there must be a means by which to address the individual agendas that affect the decision-making process of the Security Council. There must be greater transparency of process including the history of the use of the veto by the P5. This may help expedite decision making in regards to necessary humanitarian intervention.

I have become a great believer in the effectiveness of the open flow of information. This ever worldlier population would have great difficulty believing in a Security Council whose criteria for making the important decisions of our time are shrouded in secrecy.

If the UN is to maintain legitimacy, its membership must be more reflective of the modern world, with representation from countries like Japan and Germany, which were excluded in 1945, and from the developing world. There must be greater transparency of process and accountability for the decisions taken that stand in the way of peace-building initiatives. We have heard over and over that we can never allow for another Rwanda, and yet it is taking place as we speak in Darfur.

The history of the UN is ripe with examples of successes. We can look back to the declarative resolutions of the General Assembly, the resolutions that put an end to colonialism, and set out the terms by which the transfer from colonial to independent status would take place in large parts of the world. And it became the framework and the judgment call by which the Security Council and all other agencies had to abide.

It took a lot of work, but great change often does. We have the framework for great change in *The Responsibility to Protect*. A "responsibility to protect" clearly applies to the responsibilities to stop hunger and to stop maternal mortality, to stop and provide protection for all of the world's citizens. And if the protection can't be fully supplied by individual governments, then the international community has a responsibility to step in. The "responsibility to protect" and the development agenda are so closely entwined that they appear a seamless fold of the same page.

The members of the Security Council, permanent and otherwise, are entrusted with furthering these agendas, not in hindering their progress. Perhaps criteria for selection to the Security Council may be how well that nation's actions have reflected the tenets of these two crucial guidelines.

It seems to me that the reform package aims at ensuring this. Perhaps it is heightened optimism, but I believe that it aims even higher, that the proposed reform takes aim at extending the notion of public domain.

The Responsibility to Protect has the potential to become the guiding light for setting up a global public domain that holds individuals, corporations, international institutions and nation-states accountable to a set of standards of probity, and stewardship in fields of security, poverty, aid, trade and environment.

I believe this public space at the global level is beginning to emerge interlaced with new power centres and networks of decision making involving a much more varied set of civic actors that is made up of global citizens who believe that citizenship rights should trump market power and national sovereignty, and that there must be a basic framework of international law holding all participants in the domain accountable. This then can become the rationale for the UN reform package as it ultimately meets the test of true reform as suggested by Thomas Kuhn for paradigm change, i.e., a totally different way of seeing and acting in a borderless world, exercising the vocation of global citizenship.

16 MANAGING THE REFORM AGENDA
A CALL FOR TIMELY ACTION

Today's context differs from the one which was prevailing when the UN was founded in 1945. The membership has grown from 51 to 191 member states, the Cold War has come to an end, and we are living in a globalized and interdependent world.

As highlighted in the High-level Panel's report, the world is facing many more challenges and threats of a much more complex nature. There is a growing demand for accountability, welfare, freedom and democracy between and within nations. In addition to that, the world body itself reveals some weaknesses in its functioning as it was mentioned yesterday by Mme. Louise Fréchette, Deputy Secretary General, and right now, by Dr. Bruce Jones.

In this context, reforming the United Nations, whose value for the international community is unquestionable, far from being a simple routine exercise, has become a vital necessity. Today there is indeed general agreement that the time is ripe and favourable to carry out an effective reform of the UN.

We must respond efficiently to the many threats to peace and collective security on the one hand, and to the pressing and legitimate expectations for development needs, liberty and human dignity on the other hand. Dr. Jeffrey Sachs and Lord Hannay and right now Dr. Bruce Jones have already explained these proposals. The question is what kind of organization do we need in order to effectively tackle the challenges before us, for we have no other choice but to act collectively and without delay if we are to succeed.

The Secretary General's report of 21 March 2005 entitled, *In Larger Freedom: Toward Development, Security and Human Rights for All*, on which Dr. Bruce Jones has developed his comment, constitutes in this regard a timely and important contribution to our quest for answers. The report offers a thorough and in-depth review of the current situation and presents us with a number of ideas and proposals on which member states will have to make important decisions. This report draws largely from both the High-level Panel and the Millennium Project reports initiated by the Secretary General. Both reports were debated at length by the General Assembly in December 2004 and in January and February 2005, respectively. The discussions revealed a great deal of ideas. They also showed that given the nature and sensitivity of the issues on the table, acting thereon would require both a shared sense of urgency and a strong political will.

Hence, at stake is the question you have rightly asked us to address, namely, "how to move from *ideas to action?*" This implies that ideas alone will not be sufficient to change the way we do business at the UN. In fact, action, collective and effective action, is needed.

But what does it mean for an international organization with 191 member states, "*moving from ideas to action?*" How can their often diverging interests be reconciled and set on the course of a coherent and efficient action? In other words, what is to build up the political convergence required to perform a balanced and actionable reform? What is the appropriate methodology to reach this end?

Given the time constraint, I will just put forward some answers to those crucial questions and outline some of the steps already taken by the fifty-ninth session of the General Assembly. The High-level Plenary Meeting to be held in New York in September 2005 will coincide with the sixtieth anniversary of the United Nations. This is the time when world leaders will gather to solemnly adopt the series of decisions that would define the new role and architecture of the United Nations. Member states all agree that this will be a decisive occasion.

It is in this context that we have been engaged since the beginning of the fifty-ninth session in a continuous and active consultations process. This process is twofold. First, it aims at adopting the modalities for the organization of the High-level Plenary Meeting in September, and secondly its purpose is to ensure a framework for thorough consultations on the substantive issues before the member states.

Besides designing the practical arrangements for the meeting, the modalities include, inter alia, organizing:

- the informal interactive hearings of the civil society, non-governmental organizations and the private sector in June 2005;

- the high-level dialogue on Financing for Development from 27 to 28 June, which will be followed by the substantive session of ECOSOC and its functional committees; and
- the second world Conference of Speakers of Parliaments from 7 to 9 September 2005. The last preparatory meeting of this event, which I will attend, will take place in May in Libreville, Gabon, under the umbrella of the IPU.

Other meetings and mechanisms, such as the African Union and European Union summits, the Non-Aligned Movement (NAM) ministerial meeting and summit, the G-8 summit, and the Doha summit on Trade, will also provide important contributions to the preparatory process.

Against this background, we have set up an open, transparent and inclusive consultations process in the General Assembly to discuss the substantive issues before us. As I pointed out before, the Secretary General's report will serve as a basis for the consultations that the General Assembly will carry out. During this process I will be assisted by a group of seasoned diplomats who will serve as facilitators. A majority of them are here among us.

We have identified four clusters. The first will be dealing with "freedom from want," the second "freedom from fear," the third "freedom to live in dignity" and fourth, the "imperative for collective actions to strengthen the UN." It's the same thing with different words of the High-level Panel. They call it first "peace and security," second "development," third "state of law and protection of the vulnerable" and the fourth with the "UN for the twenty-first century."

At the end of this round of consultations, I envisage to submit to the member states a draft outcome document by early June. Around that time, we should be in a position to engage in further in-depth consultations, with a view to reaching the broadest possible agreement. Of course, we will have to make full use of the very limited time before us, since there is no room for any formal Preparatory Committee (Prepcom) mechanism.

Let me also stress that our work in New York will not take place in isolation. For our efforts to be productive we will need the active involvement of the respective capitals and public opinion at large, so that we make concerted and coherent progress. In this regard, we welcome the decision taken by the Secretary General to appoint special envoys. My facilitators and I look forward to working closely with them.

To summarize, I wish to emphasis the following three points: First, we need to share a sense of urgency and responsibility to act. Second, we need to engage in a spirit of cooperation and constructive dialogue. Third, we should focus on the many challenges and threats facing humanity and decide on the most effective set of measures to tackle them.

We are now at a turning point. Member states are the corner stones of the new house we want to build for the present and the future of humanity. They should not become the stumbling blocks of the reform of the United Nations. For beyond adapting the United Nations to the twenty-first century, what is really at stake here are the lives of millions of people around the world, all of whom are part of the global village.

I hope that the outcomes of this conference will make a valuable contribution to the discussions ahead.

CONCLUSION

17 THE WAY FORWARD

At a time of historical amnesia, strategic myopia, and diplomatic inertia, we need to remind ourselves why the United Nations exists in the first place and why it is still important. We need to go back to first principles, to review why the world needs a system of collective security based on the rule of law and why the United Nations is at the heart of that system. Most basically, we need to remember what the world looked like before Woodrow Wilson and Franklin Roosevelt and the other architects of multilateral cooperation created the system they did.

A hundred years ago, the only protection against aggression was power. The only checks on would-be aggressors were the costs of fighting and the risks of failing. The issue was not law; it was ambition, and capacity. Alliances emerged to deter aggression but ultimately collapsed and catastrophic conflict followed. In World War I, as armies democratized and war industrialized, ten million people died. In World War II, with technology advancing, sixty million people died. In World War III, with the advent of sophisticated weapons of mass destruction, especially nuclear weapons, how many people would die?

The generation that fought and survived the last world war, my parent's generation, knew that World War III could not be won, in any reasonable meaning of winning, and must never be fought. There had to be a better way and that better way was the United Nations and collective security. Unlike the creators of the League of Nations, the architects of the UN were determined that this time security would be assured by combining both power and principle. The United States, then as now the militarily dominant country, would be a founding member and the other major powers would likewise be present at the creation; all would contribute actively to international peace and security. The world would prevent war cooperatively, where it could, and prosecute war, collectively, where it must. At least equally important, the UN would help the world develop new norms and standards of international behaviour.

The aspirations for United Nations exceeded its grasp but it has nevertheless served us well in the intervening period, far better than its critics realize or admit. The UN gave birth to a body of international law that stigmatized aggression and created a strong norm against it. Although the Cold War saw international law breached by both sides, the norm against aggression was much more respected than not, as was the legal force of the Charter. There were fewer interstate wars in the second half of the twentieth century than in the first half, despite a nearly four-fold increase in the number of states. While the Cold War destroyed the post-war consensus, hobbling the security vocation of the UN for many years, and the prevention of World War III owed at least as much to nuclear deterrence and collective defence through NATO, there is no doubt that the world would have been a much bloodier place in the last fifty years without the world body. The UN gave birth to new concepts such as peacekeeping that provided a buffer between protagonists, so that inter-state wars did not reignite. It helped the two heavily armed camps avoid a nuclear Armageddon by, inter alia, pioneering arms control treaties and verification, notably, the Non-Proliferation Treaty regime. That regime has made us all safer by limiting the numbers of nuclear-armed states, current challenges to the IAEA notwithstanding.

The success of the United Nations has gone far beyond its security vocation. The UN has served as a midwife at the births of 140 new countries. It has contributed importantly to stability and to the process of trade and economic development, and intellectual globalization, which have delivered a period of economic growth and technological advancement unparalleled in history, undoubted excesses and inequities notwithstanding. It has created a body of human rights and humanitarian law that, as it has been progressively written into the laws of states, helped an increasing share of the world's people live in dignity and freedom. It has virtually invented the idea of sustainable development, reconciling the once polar opposites of economic growth and environmental protection.

It has fed the world's hungry, sheltered its dispossessed, ministered to its sick and educated its children. UNICEF has inoculated 575 million children against childhood diseases. The UNHCR has housed fifty million refugees and internally displaced people over the years, seventeen million people last year. The UN Mine Action Service has assisted states party to the Ottawa Treaty in their destruction of 37.5 million stockpiled landmines. The World Food Program fed 100 million people in 2003 alone. The UN Office for the Coordination of Humanitarian Affairs coordinated the massive international relief operation after the December 2004 Asian tsunami.

More mundanely, the UN has regulated the world's air travel, coordinated its mail services, protected its patents, overseen its shipping and apportioned its electromagnetic spectrum, among many other unsung but necessary tasks. From the MDGs to the terrorism conventions, to the non-proliferation regime, to environmental protection treaties, to human rights conventions, to the spread of democracy, the UN has been indispensable. To take just one example, with the creation of the International Criminal Court, the world's monsters can no longer sleep soundly in the confidence that they are immune to prosecution for abusing their own peoples, or others. The truly extraordinary contribution of the UN has been recognized eight times with Nobel Peace prizes.

Sixty years is, nevertheless, a long time in the lives of institutions, as it is in the lives of people. Through the vicissitudes of time, the UN has not kept up with change nor lived up to all of our expectations. In fact, there have been distressing inadequacies. The behaviour of the Human Rights Commission, where in Alice-in-Wonderland-like sessions perpetrators condemn others and escape censure themselves, would be funny were it not so tragic for the victims of the abuses. The Commission casts a major embarrassing shadow over the entire United Nations.

Worse have been the conscience-shocking failures. Cambodia, the Congo, and Bosnia are indelible stains on the soul of the world body. In Rwanda, even as 800,000 people were being systematically slaughtered, the Security Council played word-games about genocide, preferring to talk of "acts of genocide," taking care not to trigger the obligation under the Genocide Convention to intervene in the slaughter. Unbelievably, the Council's response to the frantic pleas of the UN commander on the ground for reinforcements was to withdraw some of his troops, when even a modest addition would have allowed him to save countless lives.

For all the subsequent remorse, not much has changed since. Now, it is Darfur that appeals to our collective conscience. What hope do ordinary people have when the Council takes refuge in the complexities of sovereignty, ethnicity, religion and economic interest to avoid acting? Meanwhile thousands upon thousands continue to die.

The UN's failures, humanity's failures, take many other forms. The lethal combination of poverty and disease kills millions a year, including children before their fifth birthdays, and small arms destroy 300,000 lives a year worldwide, mocking efforts to end conflict and rebuild states in Africa and elsewhere. Poverty traps rob the poor of their potential in vast stretches of the world, while the unfulfilled promises of assistance by some donor countries and the graft of some host governments combine to preserve the status quo. New issues arise, notably fundamentalism and the potentially catastrophic combination of terrorism and weapons of mass destruction which, rather than eliciting a cooperative response, tempt the powerful to go it alone and the weak to turn a blind eye, jeopardizing as they do so the very essence of collective security.

FIXING THE UNITED NATIONS

Some are oblivious or indifferent to the UN's weaknesses, trusting to fate to fix them. Others would just forsake the UN altogether and look to their own strengths in a dangerous age. The first course would condemn the UN to an existence increasingly on the periphery of humanity's vast need. The second course would condemn the world to repeat history in infinitely more dangerous circumstances.

The wiser course is to embrace the vision presented by the Secretary General and to adapt the institution that our parents bequeathed to us so that it serves our own times and safeguards our children's future. The place to start is to recognize that while consensus is lacking on these major questions it can be built. What is needed is not easy: to couple the Secretary General's vision with member states' political will, which history shows is not readily mobilized in the absence of a major stimulus such as the appalling experience of the Second World War.

The challenge is, therefore, to rise above the instinct, especially among UN Permanent Representatives, to conduct business as usual. The reform of the UN cannot, in any case, be left to diplomats alone. The world needs its leaders to take command of this issue. Leaders have it in their power to surmount interstate differences and to respond to the very great expectations of people around the globe. The Charter speaks of "We, the Peoples," not we the Permanent Representatives, or we the Ministers, or even we the Presidents and Prime Ministers. Leaders hold a sacred trust on behalf of their citizens. On UN reform, it is time to acquit that trust.

The Secretary General has proposed a package approach, in recognition that generating agreement inevitably entails give and take, of about sixty proposals, boiled down into four categories. Pursuant to the discussions in Waterloo and elsewhere, there appear to be a handful of truly transformative innovations that, with the requisite statesmanship, are within reach:

1. the adoption of the 0.7 percent ODA timetable and the "Quick Win" development strategy
2. the creation of an International Financial Facility
3. adoption of the emerging norm of the "responsibility to protect"
4. endorsing guidelines on the use of force
5. adopting the definition of terrorism
6. embracing the IAEA Additional Protocol
7. creating the Peacebuilding Commission
8. transforming the Human Rights Commission into a Council
9. establishing a Democracy Fund
10. undertakings of self-limiting recourse to the veto by the Permanent Members

Taken together, and with sufficiently astute diplomacy and statecraft, these ideas would go a long way towards equipping the UN to cope with the challenges it faces in the twenty-first century. The temptation to engage in invidious reductive negotiations, to find the lowest common denominator, must be avoided.

Effective reform of the UN requires more of its member states than it does of the institution itself. The message to members is simple and direct. These are not normal times. Business as usual will not do. Seize the opportunity, which might not come again soon.

In 1945, our parents were realists. They knew that the world might not survive another worldwide cataclysm. They knew that principle unsupported by power was unavailing and that power unconstrained by principle could have catastrophic consequences. They understood that cooperation would serve them well and confrontation would serve them ill, that united the world could stand, and would progress, and divided it could, and undoubtedly would, fall. We owe them a scarcely fathomable debt of gratitude for what they accomplished.

When the history of our times is written, let it be said of today's statesmen and women that they met the challenge they faced, surmounted their differences, seized the moment and transformed the United Nations. The people of the world are, literally, depending on it.

NOTES ON CONTRIBUTORS

Lloyd Axworthy is the President of the University of Winnipeg and a Special Envoy of the United Nations Secretary General to facilitate a peaceful resolution to the dispute between Ethiopia and Eritrea. Mr. Axworthy has been Minister of Foreign Affairs of Canada and a Member of Canadian Parliament. He has also served as Minister of Employment and Immigration and Minister of Transport. He has won the CARE International Humanitarian Award and was nominated for the Nobel Peace Prize for his work in the campaign for the elimination of anti-personnel landmines.

Nitin Desai is Honorary Professor at the Indian Council for Research in International Economic Relations, New Delhi, India, and Visiting Fellow at the Centre for the Study of Global Governance at the London School of Economics and Political Science, London, UK. Formerly, he held the position of Under-Secretary General for Economic and Social Affairs at the UN.

Jayantha Dhanapala is a former UN Under-Secretary General for Disarmament Affairs (1998–2003) and a former Ambassador of Sri Lanka to the US (1995–1997). He is currently a Senior Adviser to the President of Sri Lanka and Secretary General of the Secretariat for the Co-ordinating of the Peace Process.

Tom Farer is the Dean of the Graduate School of International Studies at the University of Denver. He is also the former President of the Inter-American Commission on Human Rights of the Organization of American States and of the University of New Mexico. He is an Honorary Professor of Peking University and permanent Guest Professor of People's

University and Director of the Center for China-United States Coopera-
tion. He has served as special assistant first to the General Counsel of the
Department of Defense and then to the Assistant Secretary of State for
Inter-American Affairs.

Shepard Forman is Director of the Center on International Cooperation
at New York University. Prior to founding the Center, he directed the
Human Rights and Governance and International Affairs programs at
the Ford Foundation. He has served on the faculty at Indiana University,
the University of Chicago and the University of Michigan; conducted field
research in Brazil and East Timor; and authored two books on Brazil
and numerous articles, including papers on humanitarian assistance
and post-conflict reconstruction assistance.

Louise Fréchette is the Deputy Secretary General of the United Nations.
She was Canadian Deputy Minister of National Defence from 1995 to
1998 and Associate Deputy Minister in the Department of Finance. She
served as Permanent Representative of Canada to the United Nations
from 1992 to 1995.

Patricia Goff is Assistant Professor of Political Science at Wilfrid Laurier
University and Special Research Fellow at the Centre for International
Governance Innovation. She is co-editor with Kevin C. Dunn of *Identity
and Global Politics* (Palgrave, 2004).

Lord David Hannay is a member of the House of Lords. He sat on the
United Nations High-level Panel on Threats, Challenges and Change.
He served as Permanent Representative of the United Kingdom to the
United Nations and United Kingdom Special Envoy to Cyprus. He has
served as Minister at the British Embassy in Washington, Ambassador
and Permanent Representative to the European Community (EC), Chef
de Cabinet for Sir Christopher Soames (Vice-President of the Commission of the EC), Assistant Under-Secretary of State (European Community) at the Foreign Office, and first secretary of the UK negotiating team
for entry into the EC.

Paul Heinbecker is Distinguished Research Fellow at the Centre for International Governance Innovation and Director of the Laurier Centre for
Global Relations, Governance and Policy. He was Canada's Ambassador
to the UN (2000-2003), where he supported the creation of the International Criminal Court and advocated for compromise on Iraq. Previous
positions include chief foreign policy advisor to Canadian Prime Minister Mulroney, Ambassador to Germany, and Minister in Washington.

Bruce Jones is Deputy to the Special Advisor on Follow-up on the UN High-level Panel on Threats, Challenges and Change. In 2004, he served as Deputy Research Director for the High-level Panel on Threats, Challenges and Change, in addition to being Deputy Director for the Center on International Cooperation at New York University. He was previously Chief of staff in the UN's political mission in the Middle East, and held other UN assignments in Kosovo and New York. He has written extensively on peacekeeping and post-conflict operations.

Keith Krause is Professor of International Politics at the Graduate Institute of International Studies in Geneva, and, since 1999, Director of its Programme in Strategic and International Security Studies. He is the founder and Programme Director of the Small Arms Survey project, and has jointly edited its annual yearbook since 2001.

Edward Luck is the Director of the Center on International Organization of the School of International and Public Affairs, Columbia University. For 10 years (1984-1994), Dr. Luck served as the President and CEO of the United Nations Association of the USA (UNA-USA), America's principal centre for public education on the world organization, and he subsequently served for four years as the President Emeritus of the organization (1994-1998). From December 1995 through July 1997, Dr. Luck played a key role in the United Nations reform process as a Senior Consultant to the Department of Administration and Management of the United Nations and as a Staff Director of the General Assembly's Open-ended High-level Working Group on the Strengthening of the United Nations System.

John W. McArthur is the Manager of the UN Millennium Project and Associate Director of the Earth Institute at Columbia University. With Jeffrey Sachs, he led the production of the UN Millennium Project's final report, *Investing in Development: A Practical Plan to Achieve the Millennium Development Goals*, which was co-authored by the Project's Task Force Coordinators and members of the secretariat. He is co-editor, with Michael Porter, Jeffrey D. Sachs, Peter Cornelius and Klaus Schwab, of the *Global Competitiveness Report 2001-2002*.

Jean Ping is the President of the fifty-ninth session of the United Nations General Assembly. Mr. Ping has held a variety of appointments at the ministerial level, including Ministre d'État, Minister for Foreign Affairs, Cooperation and la Francophonie, Minister of Mines, Energy and Water Resources and deputy minister in the Ministry of

Finance, Economy, Budget and Privatization, and Minister of Planning, Environment and Tourism. He has received numerous honours, both at home and abroad. He is a member of the French National Association of Doctors of Economics (ANDESE), he holds a doctorate in economics from the University of Paris I (Panthéon-Sorbonne), and he has received honorary doctorates from the Institute of Diplomacy of China and the Institute of African Studies of the Russian Academy of Sciences in Moscow.

Kenneth Roth is the Executive Director of Human Rights Watch, a post he has held since 1993. The largest US-based international human rights organization, Human Rights Watch investigates, reports on, and seeks to curb human rights abuses in some 70 countries. From 1987 to 1993, Mr. Roth served as deputy director of the organization. Previously, he was a federal prosecutor for the US Attorney's Office for the Southern District of New York and the Iran-Contra investigation in Washington.

Jeffrey Sachs is the Director of The Earth Institute, Quetelet Professor of Sustainable Development, and Professor of Health Policy and Management at Columbia University. He is Director of the UN Millennium Project and Special Advisor to United Nations Secretary General Kofi Annan on the Millennium Development Goals. Sachs is internationally renowned for advising governments in Latin America, Eastern Europe, the former Soviet Union, Asia and Africa on economic reforms and for his work with international agencies to promote poverty reduction, disease control, and debt reduction of poor countries. He was recently named among the 100 most influential leaders in the world by Time Magazine.

Ramesh Thakur is the Senior Vice Rector of the United Nations University (UNU) and Assistant Secretary General of the United Nations. He was Professor of International Relations and Director of Asian Studies at the University of Otago in New Zealand and Professor and Head of the Peace Research Centre at the Australian National University in Canberra before joining UNU in 1998. He was a Commissioner on the International Commission on Intervention and State Sovereignty which published the report *The Responsibility to Protect*, and Senior Advisor on Reforms and Principal Writer of the UN Secretary General's second reform report.

APPENDIX
CONFERENCE AGENDA

THE UN: ADAPTING TO THE TWENTY-FIRST CENTURY, WATERLOO, ONTARIO, APRIL 3–5, 2005

April 3, 2005

17:00 Public Lecture, Perimeter Institute, 31 Caroline Street, Waterloo, Ontario

17:15 Welcome by **Dr. Howard Burton**, Perimeter Institute

Introduction of the Keynote lecturer by **Dr. Michael Doyle**, Columbia University, Chairman of the Academic Council on the United Nations System (ACUNS)

Public Lecture by **Ms. Louise Fréchette**, Deputy Secretary General of the United Nations

Thank You by **Mr. Jim Balsillie**, Co-CEO of Research in Motion, Inc. and Chairman of the Board of the Centre for International Governance Innovation (CIGI)

19:00 Opening Reception and Dinner, the Centre for International Governance Innovation, 57 Erb Street West, Waterloo

Official Welcome to the Centre for International Governance Innovation by **Dr. John English**, Executive Director

Introduction to the Conference by **Mr. Paul Heinbecker**, Distinguished Fellow, Centre for International Governance Innovation and Director, Laurier Centre for Global Relations, Governance and Policy

April 4, 2005

09:00   Welcome by **Dr. Robert Rosehart**, President, Wilfrid Laurier
University

SESSION ONE: From Ideas to Action: The Reports of the UN
High Level Panel, the Millennium Project and the UN
Secretary General
Senate and Board Chamber, Wilfrid Laurier University

Moderator: **Ambassador Thomas Pickering**, Senior Vice-
President, Boeing Corp.

Dr. Jeffrey Sachs, Director, Earth Institute, Columbia University (by video)

Lord David Hannay, Member, United Nations High Level
Panel on Threats, Challenges and Change

Dr. Bruce Jones, Senior Consultant, Office of the Special
Advisor on Follow-up to the High Level Panel Report,
United Nations

H.E. Mr. Jean Ping, President of the United Nations General
Assembly

General Discussion

11:30   SESSION TWO: Rebuilding the Security Council
−13:00

Moderator: **H.E. Mr. Adolfo Aguilar Zinser,** Mexico

The UN Security Council: Reform or Enlarge?
Dr. Edward Luck, Columbia University

Discussant: **Dr. David Malone**, Assistant Deputy Minister,
Foreign Affairs Canada

General Discussion

13:00   Lunch, Paul Martin Centre

Introduction by **Dr. Jennifer Welsh**, Oxford University

Keynote Address by **Dr. Lloyd Axworthy**, former Minister
of Foreign Affairs, Canada

Thank You by **Dr. Andrew Cooper**, University of Waterloo
and CIGI

April 4 (Cont'd)

15:00   SESSION THREE: Freedom from Fear

       Moderator: **Mr. Danilo Turk,** Assistant Secretary-General for Political Affairs, United Nations

       Legal and Legitimate Use of Force under the UN Charter
       Dr. Tom Farer, University of Denver

       Discussant: **H.E. John Dauth,** Australia

       Freedom from Fear: Effective, Efficient and Equitable Security
       Dr. Ramesh Thakur, Senior Vice Rector, UN University, Tokyo

       Discussant: **Dr. Thomas Weiss,** the CUNY Graduate Center

       General Discussion

17:15   SESSION FOUR: Embracing the Reciprocal Dynamic of
–19:00   Development and Security

       Moderator: **Dr. Colin Bradford,** Brookings Institute

       The Monterrey Consensus: Developing the Policy Innovations
       Mr. Nitin Desai, London School of Economics

       Finding the Political Will: More Money, Better Governance or Both?
       Dr. John W. McArthur, Project Manager, UN Millennium Project

       Discussant: **H.E. Christopher Hackett,** Barbados and **H.E. Nana Effah-Apenteng,** Ghana

       General Discussion

19:45   Dinner Address

       The Atrium, Science Building, Wilfrid Laurier University

       Introduction by **H.E. Allan Rock,** Canada

       Speaker: **Mr. Kenneth Roth,** Executive Director, Human Rights Watch, New York

       Commentary by **H.E. Iftekhar Chowdhury,** Bangladesh and **H.E. Roman Kirn,** Slovenia

       Question and Answers

April 5, 2005

09:00   SESSION FIVE: Peace and Security; Making Collective
–11:00   Security Work for Everyone in a World of New
         Threats and Enduring Dangers

   Moderator: **Dr. Fen Hampson**

   *WMD and Terrorism: Can the UN Help to Keep the Genie in
   the Bottle?*
   Mr. Jayantha Dhanapala, Secretary General of the Peace
   Secretariat, Sri Lanka

   Discussant: **Dr. Wesley Wark**, University of Toronto

   Small Arms, Big Killers: Making the Third World Safe, Too
   Dr. Keith Krause, Graduate Institute of International
   Studies, Geneva

   Discussant: **Dr. Ernie Regehr**, Project Ploughshares

   General Discussion

11:15   SESSION SIX: Teaching an Old Dog New Tricks
–12:30
   Moderator: **Mr. Richard Stanley**, the Stanley Foundation

   *Working Better Together: Implementing the High-level Panel's
   Recommendations on Peacekeeping*
   Dr. Shepard Forman, New York University

   Discussant: **H.E. Dirk Jan van den Berg**, Netherlands,
   H.E. Ricardo Alberto Arias, Panama
   Mr. Stewart Patrick, Centre for Global Development

13:15   SESSION SEVEN: Lunch
         Summary and Outcomes

   Mr. Paul Heinbecker, Director, International Relations and
   Communication Program, CIGI and, Director, Laurier
   Centre for Global Relations, Governance and Policy